D1483030

Observing Children in Their Natural Worlds:
A Methodological Primer

Observing Children in Their Natural Worlds:
A Methodological Primer

Anthony D. Pellegrini
University of Georgia

1996

LAWRENCE ERLBAUM ASSOCIATES, PUBLISHERS
Mahwah, New Jersey

NORTHWEST MISSOURI STATE
UNIVERSITY LIBRARY
MARYVILLE, MO 64468

Copyright © 1996 by Lawrence Erlbaum Associates, Inc.
All rights reserved. No part of this book may be reproduced in
any form, by photostat, microform, retrieval system, or any other
means, without the prior written permission of the publisher.

Lawrence Erlbaum Associates
10 Industrial Avenue
Mahwah, New Jersey 07430

cover design by Gail Silverman

Library of Congress Cataloging-in-Publication Data

Observing children in their natural worlds : a methodological primer
／ Anthony D. Pellegrini.
        p. cm.
Includes bibliographical references and index.
ISBN 0-8058-2152-X (pbk. : alk. paper)
1. Behavioral assessment of children. 2. Child psychology—
Research—Methodology. 3. Observation (Psychology) 4.
Observation (Educational method)   I. Title.
BF722.P45 1996
155.4'0723—dc20

95-39718
CIP

Books published by Lawrence Erlbaum Associates are printed on
acid-free paper, and their bindings are chosen for strength and durability.

Printed in the United States of America
10 9 8 7 6 5 4 3 2 1

155.4
P380

MAR 05 1997

CONTENTS

PREFACE

MY ORIENTATION

This is a book about ways in which to conduct observations. Observational methods are a set of research tools that are useful in describing and explaining behaviors and interactions of children and adults alike. Indeed, the methods presented here are drawn from disciplines such as anthropology, psychology, sociology, and education, whose aim is to describe people's interactions in settings as varied as schools, bus queues, and dinner conversations. I draw extensively from the ethological literature, which provides thorough and careful methods for observing animals in their natural habitats. In short, in this book I draw on various academic disciplines to provide a set of procedures that are useful in helping us describe interactions. Although I draw upon various disciplines in my discussions, I am primarily concerned with children and adults in school and family settings.

Behavioral observations are useful to students of many sorts. Observations can be used to describe children's interactions either in an experimental laboratory or on the school playground. In this book I am concerned primarily with more naturalistic settings. In settings such as schools, observational methods are useful for designing and evaluating programs for teachers and students. Naturalistic observations are particularly useful in light of the current criticisms of tests used to evaluate children and teachers. Observational methods are powerful tools in describing children and adults in the situations in which they function every day. Educators reading this book should consider observations as basic assessment tools.

My orientation in outlining observational methods is to stress the interrelation between behavior/interaction and the context in which it occurs. Thus, I stress conducting observations in such a way that the behavior of individuals is related to the physical and social contexts in which it occurs. This means that we describe not only the behaviors and interactions of a focal person but also the location of the interactions and the behavior of other participants as they relate to the focal person. Such an orientation, I believe, helps us explain why some children exhibit high levels of social competence in one setting, such as interacting with peers in the playground, while exhibiting lower levels of social competence in other settings, such as interacting with teachers during reading lessons.

Consistent with this orientation of describing behavior and interaction in relation to context, in this book I discuss in great detail the importance of conducting observations in everyday settings, like homes, schools, and child care centers. Although these methods can obviously be used to describe behaviors in either the field (i.e., the natural world) or in an experimental laboratory, I spend considerably more time on the former. I suggest that in order to understand behaviors and interaction patterns we must situate them in contexts in which they actually develop and occur; behaviors and interaction patterns and contexts co-adapt to each other.

There are, generally, two orientations that can be followed in describing behavior in context: the insider and the outsider orientation. The insider orientation, with roots in ethnography and ethnomethodology, tries to describe behavior and interaction qualitatively or interpretatively from the perspective of the participants. To this end, observers are often participant observers to the extent that they try to take some role within the group being observed. Furthermore, the insider approach often utilizes data analysis techniques that have been labeled qualitative, interpretive, and contrastive. This technique analyzes observational data by putting them into categories that differ in terms of the function they serve. This form of analysis is in contrast to describing behaviors in terms of degree. In the latter case, behaviors are considered different in terms of quantity rather than in terms of kind.

Although the outsider approach, with its roots in ethology and psychology, often analyses behaviors and interaction in terms of quantity (or degree), it too tries to gain an insider's understanding on the phenomena under observation. Like the ethnographer and ethnomethodologist, the ethologist and the ecological psychologist aim to understand behavior from the perspective of the participants. They, however, do not use participant observation techniques. Instead, they observe participants and their cohorts in various natural situations.

In this book I discuss and outline assumptions and methods associated primarily with the outsider perspective, though the insider perspective is discussed by way of contrast. Indeed I discuss in detail decision points that are helpful in choosing a perspective. The primary orientation of this book is consistent with methods and analytical techniques associated with the outsider perspective.

THE CONTENTS OF THIS BOOK

My aim in writing this book was to provide a source that would serve as a guide or handbook of sorts for students and researchers who are unfamiliar with observational methods. As noted previously, these methods are useful to educators concerned with assessing children and teachers as well as to researchers. Indeed, I hope that educators and researchers use this book in similar ways. Both researchers and educators are concerned with the process of asking and answering specific questions. Observational methods presented in this volume can be useful in solving basic scientific problems and can be useful for the practitioner, presented with a problem and searching for a set of tools to solve the problem. This book is concerned primarily with using the scientific method and observational methods to solve everyday problems. Indeed, I believe that the distinction between basic and applied research is an artificial one to the extent that scientists gain insight into basic processes by studying everyday phenomena. To this end, chapters are arranged in a sequence from initially choosing to use observational methods to final discussions of data analysis. The organization of the book thus follows what I think is a reasonable sequence involved in this process. Given my child developmental and educational background, I aimed the book at students conducting research in applied settings, such as schools, hospitals, clinics, and homes.

At the end of each chapter there are two sorts of study guides: Things to Think About and a Glossary. Both of these guides were designed to help the reader better understand the material presented in the chapter. Further completion of these exercises should aid you in the use of the material for conducting "real" observations. To these ends, I recommend that these exercises be completed after reading each chapter.

In Chapter 1, I begin with a discussion of the importance of observational methods. In this chapter I discuss reasons for initially choosing to use observational techniques rather than other techniques, such as questionnaire or testing. Generally, the value of observational methods relate to the descriptions they provide. Good descriptions are defined as reliable and valid; that is, the degree to which they are consistent and truthful. Such descriptions, I suggest, are important in their own right to the extent that they help us understand clearly what it is we are studying. By putting behaviors into categories we, by direct implication, understand them more fully than before they were categorized to the extent that we view the behaviors in terms of other categories. These descriptions provide a necessary basis for causal explanations. That is, clear descriptions of behaviors are a necessary starting point for understanding which behaviors elicit other behaviors.

In Chapter 2, I outline two perspectives on observational methods: the insider perspective and the outsider perspective. This distinction is basic in conducting observational research. Students and researchers must choose their perspective because specific methods follow from this basic choice. For example, choosing an insider perspective has the direct implication of choosing participant observational techniques. Correspondingly, choice of an outsider perspective necessitates the use of nonparticipant observational techniques.

In Chapter 3, we get closer to the actual process of conducting an observation by making more choices. The most salient choice relates to observing in a laboratory or the field. With this choice made, the observer must next consider ways in which to maximize the objectivity of his or her techniques. Issues of bias and replication are discussed here. In relation to the objectivity issue, some guidelines are provided for when to conduct observations (that is, what part of the day) and how much data to collect (that is, number of observations). These last issues help guarantee that the data we collect represent in some way a reasonable sample of participants' behaviors in specific contexts.

In Chapter 4, I discuss initial entry into the field. By the field I mean the setting where observations will actually be conducted, such as a playground, a classroom, or a household. In this critical phase of the observational process, observers enter the field with their basic research question in mind. In the process of these preliminary observations, observers refocus their question more clearly in light of what they observe. They also consider the logistics of conducting systematic observations to answer this question in this specific setting. An important aspect of this preliminary phase is the formation of behavioral categories; this process is discussed in great detail in Chapter 5.

In Chapter 5, discussion revolves around different ways of categorizing behavior and interaction and developing categories that are relevant to a specific project.

Chapter 6 is a very specific discussion of collecting data on the categories that were defined in Chapter 5. A group of sampling and recording rules that govern the observational plan are outlined. These rules tell us when and how to observe. Sampling and recording rules are necessary guides to the collection of representative and objective information. The units of analyses corresponding to specific choices are also outlined.

In Chapter 7, I continue to discuss methods for maximizing objectivity. Specifically, I discuss establishing and checking on the reliability and validity of the data organized into behavioral categories. Different forms of reliability and validity are discussed. Additionally, ways of testing each are outlined.

In Chapter 8, I discuss ways in which categories can be counted. Specifically, I discuss issues related to independence of measurement in units of analyses. Independence of units of analysis is crucial if statistical procedures are to be used appropriately.

Chapter 9 is an elementary discussion of descriptive and inferential statistical techniques used to organize the observational data collected. The aim of this chapter is simply to expose the reader to some basic statistical tenets, not to provide an exhaustive or authoritative guide to statistical analyses of behavioral data. Some of the more basic but useful procedures, such as standard deviations and sign tests, are outlined specifically.

Chapter 10 is rather like a mail-order catalogue of technologies that can be used to record behavior. The technologies range from paper and pencil techniques, like checklists and narratives, to computerized event recorders.

Chapter 11 is a departure from the direct observational techniques outlined in the book. In this chapter I discuss indirect observational methods, such as spot sampling and rating scales. These techniques are useful for obtaining information that is very difficult to obtain via direct observation; for example, spot observations can be used in describing where and with whom children spend their time after school.

In Chapter 12, I discuss the uses of observational data for children in educational settings. I suggest that descriptions of children in their everyday environments can be useful in developing educational programs. Further observational techniques are very useful in the evaluation of educational programs. The particular value of using observational data for evaluation, compared to information provided by paper and pencil testing, is that it captures children and teachers in natural and, I hope, motivating contexts. This aspect of observational methods should, in turn, help us more accurately assess levels of competence. Children and adults alike exhibit higher levels of competence in situations that they view as meaningful and motivating, compared to less meaningful and motivating situations.

In the end, this book is about using observational methods to understand the behaviors and interaction patterns that typify the worlds of those we wish to study. In order to work most effectively in these worlds, we should understand what the participants are doing in these worlds. Observational descriptions are necessary for our understanding of children and the worlds in which they live.

ACKNOWLEDGMENTS

Acknowledgments in most books read like familiar scripts, where we thank and acknowledge lots of different people for various things. Similarly the authors accept responsibility for shortcomings of the book. In this acknowledgment I follow this time-honored script. First, the idea of doing this book came from my work in children's playground behavior and human ethology. The observational methods utilized in this literature were a very important part of its appeal. My collaboration with P. K. Smith in this area has been most instructive. Additionally, Craig Hart and Everett Waters read early drafts of this book and provided valuable comments.

Additionally, the comments of students in my child study course and my observational methods course must be acknowledged. They first heard and read the ideas presented here. Also, I thank Lee Galda for help in areas too numerous to mention, but I outline a few very specific cases. Her suggestions on ways to make this book more student friendly were always in the foreground as I wrote and rewrote.

Financial support was provided so that I could spend two quarters working on the manuscript. Support from the National Reading Research Center and the Institute for Behavioral Research, both at the University of Georgia, is much appreciated. Additionally, G. M. A. Stanic, my department head in Early Childhood Education at Georgia, was always there with resources (e.g., when my computer died) and encouragement to develop a course on observational methods. Lastly, the financial and collegial support provided by the Graduate School of Education and the Centre for Child and Family Studies at Leiden University must be acknowledged. Specifically, the initiatives of A. Bus and M. van Ijzendoorn enabled me and my family to spend the summer in Leiden and work on this book in the most hospitable and supportive conditions.

Anthony D. Pellegrini

1

Why Use Observational Methods?

USES OF DESCRIPTION

In this book I am concerned with using observational methods, primarily in everyday settings. By observational methods I mean methods that are based on direct observations of behavior. These methods are, in turn, helpful in describing the behavior of individuals and groups of individuals as they interact in real time. An important goal of this method is to provide the reader with a verbal picture of behaviors as they unfold. These descriptions are very useful for a number of important ventures, such as working with children and families at home and in school. An indispensable part of all description of behavior is a thorough explication of aspects of the contexts in which the behavior is embedded. My assumption is that behaviors are rendered understandable when they are considered in their context. Context, most generally, refers to the physical (e.g., spatial arrangements of desks in a classroom) and social dimensions (e.g., number and composition of the group being observed) of the observational setting.

Although this is a very general definition, it is useful in understanding the interrelations between individuals' behaviors and the situation in which they are embedded (see Hinde, 1976, for an exhaustive description of context). Two behaviors may have similar features but have very different meanings, depending on context. For example, the play face and gentle push of a popular child (i.e., a dimension of the social context) are typically interpreted as playful. From an aggressive child, on the other hand, the same behavior is typically interpreted as aggressive. Thus, one dimension of context, the participants, relates to the meaning of the behaviors exhibited.

Although the methods discussed in this book are generic—that is, they can be applied to the observations of ground squirrels, rhesus monkeys, shoppers in a supermarket, or children on playgrounds—I am concerned primarily with children embedded in the context of schools, neighborhoods, and families. These methods can be applied to describing children in the many contexts they inhabit. I agree fully with the concerns expressed by Herbert Wright (1960), over 30 years ago, when he noted that we have limited knowledge of children. Our knowledge now, as was the

case 30 years ago, is based mostly on descriptions of children in preschool settings or in laboratories. This concern was echoed by Bronfenbrenner (1979) 20 years after Wright, but we still know very little about children outside of school settings. For example, we know virtually nothing about who children interact with after school and on weekends. Given today's demographics of increasing instances of dual career families, single parents, and paternal custody it seems important to generate such descriptions. After all, some of our educational intervention strategies, such as joint book reading between mothers and their children, assume that this is still the primary dyad in children's lives. Observational methods applied to children's natural worlds can be very helpful in answering these sorts of applied and policy questions.

GOOD DESCRIPTIONS: MAXIMIZING
RELIABILITY AND VALIDITY

Although I suggest that the methods considered here are useful for observing children in their everyday worlds, I also note that the same observational methods can be used in experimental laboratories as well. In both cases the aim of good description is the same. Good descriptions meet the criteria of being reliable and valid. Generally, reliable observations are those in which one observer records in a consistent manner and there is agreement between different observers. Valid observations, on the other hand, are those that actually measure what they purport to measure. Much more is said about these issues in subsequent chapters (e.g., Chapter 7); suffice it to say for now that in both the laboratory and in the field reliability between and among observers is necessary but not sufficient for validity. Simply put, before we can claim anything about the truthfulness of our descriptions (i.e., validity) we must agree on what it is we see (i.e., reliability).

With validity we have the usual trinity of concerns: internal validity, external validity, and ecological validity. It is on these validity issues that laboratory and field methods diverge, and often the divergence is abrupt. Laboratory procedures are concerned primarily with internal validity and are less concerned with external validity. By manipulating and controlling variables, experimenters can make internally valid statements about the effects of independent variables (such as the nature of toys to which children are exposed) on dependent variables (such as children's play behavior). That is, we can be sure that variation in an independent variable is affecting the dependent measures. Experimenters are often less concerned with external validity, or generalizing laboratory results to relevant field settings, and ecological validity, or the comparison of results across a number of different settings.

Field studies (i.e., studies of people in their everyday environments), on the other hand, are primarily concerned with describing behavior as it occurs in its natural habitat and recognizing limited internal validity. This imbalance in both laboratory and field approaches results in incomplete knowledge. Obviously, descriptions of laboratory behavior with minimal ties to its field analogue are of limited use and interest. Similarly, descriptions of behavior in the field, without clear limits on alternative explanations, do not advance our understanding of the ways in which variables affect each other. Alternatives to these two approaches include designing ecologically valid experiments, such as comparisons of children's behavior in laboratory and classroom settings (e.g., Bronfenbrenner, 1979), or taking advantage of natural experiments. Examples of natural experiments include examining the effects of neighborhoods on juvenile delinquency by studying children who are delinquent in one area after they move to a low crime neighborhood (e.g., Rutter & Garmezy, 1983). With these two alternative approaches we have the best of both worlds: We have research conducted in the field with some degree of experimental control.

If we do not work toward some sort of rapprochement between experimental and field approaches, disciplines such as early education and both child and educational psychology are sure to atrophy, and probably with good cause. I say with good cause because our experiments should aspire to explain the ways in which organisms live and develop in their natural world. We need some level of explanation and causal inferences so that we can begin to understand these processes more clearly and then use this information to design educational environments. My bias is that description is an important and necessary first step of any scientific enterprise.

MERE DESCRIPTION?

Frequently descriptive research, in which observational methods play an indispensable part, is considered merely descriptive, implying that description is either an unimportant or an atheoretical enterprise. Mere descriptions are often contrasted with research designs that are explanatory, to the extent that the latter proffers causal statements for the interrelation among variables. I, along with others (e.g., Blurton Jones, 1972; Hinde, 1980), believe that thorough descriptions are a necessary and very important first step in conducting research that aims to explain. Correspondingly, descriptions are important aspects of most educational programs.

Good descriptions are neither atheoretical nor less scientific than approaches offering causal explanations. The ability to describe a phenomenon adequately, especially in complex organisms like humans, requires some theory. The complexity of the human organism interacting, even in the simplest ways, necessitates that observers make choices about who, what, and when to observe. For example, take the seemingly simple issue of classifying participants' roles. Kagan's (1994) simple but informative example clearly points to the importance of theory in description: "Zoologists classify cows as mammals, economists classify them as commodities, and some cultures regard these animals as sacred symbols" (p. 11). Further, theory guides us in terms of the levels of specificity of our categories. If we had a biological orientation, we might examine relations between hormones and behavior. If we had a cultural-anthropological perspective, we might examine the match between the cultures of school tasks and those indigenous to children's homes. Given the complexity of the phenomena that can be observed, a clear theoretical orientation is necessary because it guides decisions we make about observational methods.

It thus makes sense to put in the foreground, or to make explicit, those decisions we make when we observe. In this way we know the paths we have traveled in making these decisions. It is naive and unrealistic for observers to think or state that they enter an observational field with no biases in terms of what they will observe or how the phenomena will be observed and categorized. Human observers have too many schema, or concepts about the ways in which the world works, in their heads to take such a stance. The best we can hope for is to make our biases explicit and to try to minimize them. Observers cannot go out and observe everything for there is clearly too much to observe. With this in mind, we should make explicit what it is we are interested in (that is, our question). With an explicit question in mind (which may arise from making preliminary observations) we can begin to consider what it is specifically we will observe.

USING OBSERVATIONAL METHODS IN
APPLIED CHILD STUDY

The major focus of this book is on using observational methods with children and their families. Thus, observations can be conducted in the home, school, after-school programs, and anywhere else that children spend time. I follow the child study tradition (see Pellegrini, 1992, and Chapter 12 of this book) whereby good descriptions of children are the bases for designing educational as well as other sorts of intervention programs. Thus, my basic assumption is that we must understand children before we can intervene. Observational methods are an indispensable tool used in understanding children.

There is a crucial need for good descriptions (that is, reliable and valid descriptions) of children in settings where they spend substantial portions of their time. Descriptions of this sort are useful in a number of ways. They should provide bases for programs for children and families. For examples, models of successful adult–child and child–child interaction, derived from descriptive work, can be used to design programs for teacher–child and peer interaction in schools.

The assumption that programs for children and families should be based on good descriptions of children and their families is an old one and is basic to the child study movement (see Pellegrini, 1992). The child study movement assumes that the child and the family are at the center of any educational program in which they are enrolled.

Dimensions of the programs, such as curriculum materials and teacher strategies, as well as evaluation of the program are based on these descriptions.

The child study approach to programs for children can be contrasted with other approaches to education. For example, many educational programs base their programs on the nature of the subject matter being taught; that is, rather than basing mathematics or science lessons on the nature of the child, subject approaches typically present basic subject matter concepts in a manner consistent with the disciplines.

The approach I advocate involves using observations to describe children in various stages of their educational experiences. More specifically, observations provide the bases of generating curriculum and instruction as well as evaluation procedures. Descriptions of children in their everyday context, school and non-school settings, are particularly useful here. The importance of using children's relevant everyday experiences for educational programs has been recognized for many years, most recently by Cole (1993).

Activities that are important in children's communities and family lives need to be identified and described so that they can be included in educational programs. For example, certain groups of children may experience specific interaction styles of reading and mathematics activities as important aspects of their culture (Pellegrini & Stanic, 1993). These specific activities, rather than others, are often motivating for children. The inclusion of such indigenous strategies and materials in the educational curriculum is important, particularly when the children in those programs come from culturally diverse communities. Thus, observational methods form an important part of the curriculum planning cycle.

Evaluation of children and programs is another part of the curriculum cycle for which observational methods can be very useful. By evaluation I mean documenting the operation and impact of the program. Traditionally, children and teachers have been evaluated with various forms of paper and pencil tests. For example, to document a teacher's competence to teach, some schools use tests of teachers' knowledge of subject matter. Similarly, paper and pencil tests are typically used to determine the extent to which children have mastered the subject matter presented in the programs. The criticisms of such approaches are well recognized and have been more eloquently argued elsewhere (e.g., Shepard, 1993) so I do will not restate them except to say, generally, that tests are less than perfect indicators of young children's competence.

Use of tests is particularly problematic with young children, as we have known for many years (see Messick, 1983, for a thorough discussion). One reason is that tests are artificial and sometimes anxiety-producing events; this combination of factors, as well as numerous factors related to the design of tests per se, adversely affects children's test-taking behavior. The effects of these extraneous factors on children are probably responsible for the well-known fact that children are unreliable test takers (Messick, 1983). That is, their scores on different days tend to vary. Indeed, when children and adults are placed in anxiety-producing situations, they tend to exhibit lower, rather than higher, levels of competence. This may be because that they are unwilling to offer new or novel solutions in a threatening situation. With such unreliability we have no chance for validity.

In light of these many limitations of testing, the educational community has begun to consider alternative forms of assessment, such as authentic assessment and portfolio assessment. Observational methods fit quite nicely into this movement in that they are excellent for gathering information on children and teachers in authentic situations. Consequently, observational methods are useful for evaluation of children and teachers to the extent that they do not put them in anxiety-producing situations; thus, we have a higher likelihood of getting a truer measure of their competence.

An added benefit of observational methods relates to the finding that results from naturalistic observations do not have to generalize from one performance context to another. Tests often fail to take into account performance contexts. More specifically, reliable and valid test scores are indicators of how children and teachers might perform in the contexts from which the test items were generated. Thus, the scores should generalize or transfer to a performance (i.e., real) setting. Observational methods have the benefit of documenting competence in those relevant situations from the start. If we are interested in making inferences about teachers' ability to teach literacy lessons, we can observe them directly in those sorts of lessons. We do not have to test them on subject and instructional materials related to literacy and then make inferences about teaching ability.

In order to use observational techniques effectively, however, observers must be careful to choose, or sample, behaviors and events that they see as important. A sure guide here is to observe those aspects of the program that are specified in the program goals and objectives. Based on specified program goals and objectives, the observer can, first, document the degree to which these program components are actually being implemented. Descriptions of program implementation are very important because there is often a mismatch between educational programs as they are stated in the policy manual and the actual implementation of the program. Thus, we must first describe the actual process and the degree to which it relates to the formal (or written) program. A second step in the evaluation process has the observer documenting the degree to which these program components relate to children's development. Thus, by matching specific program components with specific child outcomes, we can design effective programs.

As I discuss in later sections and chapters (specifically Chapter 12), this is no quick fix, for the use of observational methods to conduct evaluations is very time consuming. To make inferences about competence based on observations requires numerous observations, whereas less time is typically involved in testing. Thus, costs and benefits exist in both areas.

SUMMARY AND CONCLUSIONS

Observational methods are general techniques for use in either experimental or field settings. In each setting, investigators should be concerned with the dual concerns of reliability and validity; correspondingly, attention should be paid to internal, external, and ecological validity. If our goal is to use observational methods to understand the ways in which specific children and adults interact in the world, it is imperative that we attend to these issues of reliability and validity with the utmost vigilance.

The ways in which we choose to use the methods outlined in this book, of course, will vary depending on individuals' needs. Certainly this book should be useful to students of the scientific study of behavior, interactions, and relationships. It is the aim of this group to describe the interaction between organism and environment. Recollection of Wright's (1960) advice, however, should be kept in mind when we choose a problem to study. Recall, 30 years ago, he bemoaned the fact that we knew very little about children beyond the preschool period and outside of the confines of their preschool classrooms or outside the laboratory. Thirty years later, things have not changed much. If we want to understand children's circumstances it seems that a very important first step is to describe what they spend their time doing and with whom they do it. From an educational perspective, this information can be very useful in program design.

Observational methods are useful in solving problems with which we are confronted in our everyday circumstances. For example, a teacher confronted with a noncompliant child can apply these methods to begin to identify the nature of the context and the behaviors that constitute noncompliance for this specific child. These noncompliant behaviors could be paired with specific consequences in service of identifying possible motives. The work of Gerald Patterson (e.g., 1982) and colleagues is exemplary in its use of observational methods to describe the behaviors of problem children in their everyday lives. In short, this sort of action research, where a person studies a relevant problem in real-world circumstances, is very useful. Given the rather idiosyncratic nature of most problems and concerns, it seems to me that teachers, social workers, labor organizers (see R. H. Tawney's 1973 biography by Ross Terrill for an interesting example), and the like, can most effectively solve work-related problems when they confront the problems themselves.

A basic starting point, no matter what type of research venture we plan, is a thorough description of what we plan to study. As noted, descriptions are a necessary part of any scientific or intervention enterprise. Descriptions are needed to generate reliable and valid categories that help us to understand those who are being observed. Research of this sort can also be used to solve real problems people confront every day.

THINGS TO THINK ABOUT

1. Regarding the interrelation between dimensions of context and their effect on behavior, consider the following:

Sam and Jack playing together with blocks.

Sam and Jack playing together with dolls.

Sam and Anna playing together with blocks.

Sam and Anna playing together with dolls.

1a. How do you think the children would act in each situation?

_____

_____

_____

_____

_____

_____

_____

2. How do you think the behavior of children and their parents would differ if they were observed playing a board game at home versus if they were playing the same game in an experimental room?

_____

_____

_____

_____

_____

_____

_____

2a. How might you find out?

_____

_____

_____

_____

_____

_____

_____

3. Where and with whom do children that you know spend most of their out-of-school time?

_____

_____

_____

_____

_____

_____

_____

3a. How would you go about finding out?

_____

_____

_____

_____

_____

_____

_____

_____

3b. Why would such descriptions be useful?

_____

_____

_____

_____

_____

_____

_____

GLOSSARY

Child study: The orientation that studying and understanding children is necessary for the design of educational environments for children.
  Give your example:

_____

_____

_____

_____

_____

Context: A general term used to refer to those things that surround the person being observed, for example, toys, peers, room size.
Give your example:

_____

_____

_____

_____

_____

Descriptions by consequence: Describing a behavior in terms of what it leads to.
Give your example:

_____

_____

_____

_____

_____

Description, physical: Describing in terms of physical movements.
Give your example:

_____

_____

_____

_____

_____

Generalize: The degree to which data from an experiment can be applied to explaining a similar phenomenon in the real world.

Give your example:

_____

_____

_____

_____

_____

Reliability: The degree to which observations are consistent across time and agreed on by others. Reliability is necessary but not sufficient for validity.

Give your example:

_____

_____

_____

_____

_____

Validity: Generally refers to the truthfulness of the data. Internal validity refers to the degree to which inferences from experiments are truthful and the extent to which we control alternative explanations. External validity refers to the degree to which we can generalize from the laboratory to a real-world context. Ecological validity refers to the degree to which similar results occur in the laboratory and the field.

Give your example:

_____

_____

_____

_____

_____

2

Choosing a Perspective: Insider/Outsider

When we observe someone or something, we take a perspective on the phenomenon under examination. This perspective should be guided by our theoretical orientation. By making explicit our theoretical perspective, we make clear our assumptions about the phenomena under observation and can then construct a coherent plan by which questions are asked, methods are planned and implemented, data are analyzed, and results are interpreted. In short, an explicit theoretical perspective on our work serves as a guide for the whole observational project. All parts of the observation should follow from a particular perspective. In this chapter I outline my theoretical perspective on observations: the outsider perspective. By way of contrast, I discuss this perspective in relation to the insider perspective.

The insider perspective and the outsider perspective correspond, roughly, to qualitative, or interpretive and empirical, or quantitative methodologies, respectively. The specific disciplines that have pioneered observational methodologies in the interpretive area include ethnography and sociology, and more recently, literary criticism theories have been applied to theories of research. In the area of empirical theory, ethology, psychology, and child study have made important contributions to observational methods.

In this chapter I briefly outline the respective positions represented by the insider and outsider views. The intent here is to help students sort out their positions on these issues so that they can outline and then follow a consistent set of observational practices and analyses. Although both perspectives are discussed in this chapter, my orientation follows the outsider perspective. The reader interested in the interpretive approach to observational methods is referred to volumes by Fine and Sandstrom (1988) and Patton (1990). At the risk of stating the obvious, I stress that both approaches to observational study are equally rigorous. To take a simple but powerful example, Einstein's thought experiments did not involve data in the traditional sense, but they certainly met the paradigm standard of science (i.e., falsifiable hypotheses)! Each approach takes a different tack on data sources and interpretations, but both are concerned with proffering the best description of the phenomena at hand. By best description I mean descriptions that are reliable and valid.

BASIC DIFFERENCES: THE ETIC–EMIC CONTRAST

Borrowing from Sapir (1925), Hymes (1980) made a basic distinction between the qualitative or interpretive methods and quantitative approaches by noting that the former is concerned with behaviors as social signals that are embedded in a systems of other social signals. Functional contrast, not measurement of individual or isolated phenomena, is the way in which behavior is rendered meaningful for qualitative researchers. Thus, interpretive researchers are concerned with distinctions in function or meaning, not differences in degree. For example, the meaning of a specific behavior or sound in relation to other behaviors or sounds is considered. The contrastive dimension refers to determining the ways in which specific sounds or behaviors serve similar or different meaningful functions. Assigning behaviors and sounds to categories is based on their serving similar functions. Sapir's (1925) notion of the phoneme is a paradigm example of this method. In one culture two distinctive sounds may serve two very different functions, like /l/ and /r/ in English, whereas the same two sets of sounds serve the one function in another language, like Chinese. Thus, analysis is concerned with the functional differences between sounds, not measuring and quantifying the specific aspects of the sounds in /l/ and /r/.

Consider a nonlinguistic example of a specific social behavior, hitting someone with an open hand. For one group of children this behavior would be part of a playful category, labeled rough-and-tumble play; for another group of children it may belong to an aggressive category in that it leads to real fighting. The insider perspective tries to derive the ways in which specific behaviors serve different functions within a specific group. Fine examples of qualitative research, utilizing participants' observational techniques, of children's playground behavior can be found in Sluckin (1981).

Quantitative approaches, on the other hand, are typically concerned with describing and measuring isolated physical events, such as behaviors and sounds. In linguistics the distinction between the interpretive and the empirical is referred to as the emic and etic distinction (Pike, 1965). The former, corresponding to the interpretive, refers to the meaning and function assigned to a particular group of sounds, and the latter, corresponding to the quantitative, refers to the physical properties of the specific sounds. So, for example, a phonetic analysis describes certain sound properties. Thus, description is concerned primarily with measuring properties of the sounds produced. Phonemic analysis, on the other hand, reveals the extent to which different sounds have different meanings for specific groups. This distinction is represented in Fig. 2.1.

Recently, aspects of literary theory have influenced research methods generally. One such theory, derived from post modernism, posits that interpretations of events are individualist, due to a lack of an objective perspective on any event. Thus, attempts

| Outsider/etic | Quantitative | Measure discrete behavior |
| Insider/emic | Qualitative | Functional contrast |

FIG. 2.1   Perspectives on observational methods.

to reach consensus of viewing an event (in terms of interobserver reliability) are meaningless acts. The reader interested in this approach is referred to Berieter's excellent summary of post-modern though applied to educational research. It is clearly beyond the scope of the present volume.

In the remainder of this chapter I discuss the outsider perspective.

THE OUTSIDER PERSPECTIVE

The outsider perspective, in one extreme version, assumes that observers should divorce themselves entirely from any interpretation of insiders' meaning because such introspection and self-report data are too subjective and unreliable (see Blurton Jones, 1972, for a version of this position). Indeed, such assumptions are not unlike those made by behavioral psychologists, particularly in relation to their more cognitive counterparts. For example, behavioral psychologists such as B. F. Skinner (1974) were insistent that the only scientific way to describe people and other animals was behaviorally; other means were bound to fail because they were too subjective. Thus, the observer should maintain the outsider perspective so as to maximize the objective and minimize the subjective. The limitations of this strict behavioral position have been repeatedly and convincingly pointed out (e.g., see Cheyney & Seyfarth, 1990, for an interesting discussion of making cognitive inferences about social behaviors).

Methods derived from the outsider perspective were particularly useful in early studies of animal behavior and human infants, both in the field and in the laboratory. After all, when working with animals and infants it is rather difficult to interview them to gain their perspectives on events! Yet inferences about cognitive processes, such as motives and thoughts, can be made from observations of social behavior. In this regard, observers utilizing ethological methods have added considerably to our understanding of observational methods and human development. In this section, I outline two methods associated with the outsider perspective: ethology and ecological observations.

Ethology

Ethology has been described as the biological study of behavior (Cairns & Cairns, 1986; Pellegrini, 1992). Ethology is concerned with describing organisms in their natural environments. Only by rich descriptions of behaviors in their naturally occurring context can we begin to understand them. The theoretical underpinnings for this proposition relate specifically to the Darwinian origins of ethology. Following this general orientation, behavior develops and is learned by an individual in an interactive relationship with the environment; adaptation is a product of this relationship. Thus, we should try to understand the ways in which the behaviors of a specific group are interrelated with the specific characteristics of their environment. Individuals choose, adapt to, and shape their environments in ways that maximize their success in those niches. Success, from a Darwinian standpoint, refers to reproductive success.

Step 1: Exploratory observation
Step 2: Ethogram

FIG. 2.2.   Steps in ethological observation process.

Ethologists typically work from the assumption that the categories into which behaviors are placed should emerge from the data. Categories take on specific meaning depending on the contexts in which they are observed. A primary job of ethologists is to describe behavior in context; it follows that they should impose minimal structure on those behaviors in advance. Descriptive categories are induced by ethologists during the observational period. The generation of categories is very important to the hypothesis generation phase of the research enterprise. After the categories are defined and hypotheses generated they can be tested.

As in all observational and categorization enterprises, however, a question, or theory, guides the categorization and observational process. The steps in the ethologically oriented observational process are displayed in Fig. 2.2.

The observational methods used by ethologists are useful in describing those contexts in which specific events usually occur (e.g., identifying locations of desirable and undesirable child behaviors) and in determining causes and motivates for specific acts.

Categories are induced only after a period of *exploratory observation*. In this initial period of study, the observer enters the field with minimal assumptions and a priori categories about the ways in which things operate. In the course of the exploration period, the children under observation get used to the observer's presence, and the observer, in turn, begins to recognize the dynamics of the individuals being observed. During this phase, the observer should work out a number of important logistical issues. For example, the observer should determine the best times and places to conduct the observations, possible recording devices to be used, and possible behaviors of interest to be considered in a coding scheme.

After this initial period (discussed further in the next chapter), the ethologist constructs an ethogram, or a behavioral index for the children under consideration in a specific context. The importance of accurate description of behaviors in context is a necessary step in our understanding of those behaviors. In Fig. 2.3, an ethogram for elementary school children's playground behavior is displayed.

This level of description (taken from Pellegrini, 1995) is a necessary first step in understanding the behavior of focal children. Given the practical limitations of constructing detailed descriptions, ethograms for children across many different situations are very difficult; thus, we should aim to construct ethograms of focal children in contexts that are of specific interest.

The next step in the observational process for the ethologist involves *systematic observation*. Systematic observations, as the label implies, follow a specific set of rules. A basic set of theoretical assumptions that has guided ethological descriptions since its inception was put forth by one of its founders N. Tinbergen (1963). In his *Four Whys*, Tinbergen suggested that four questions should be posed in the study of behaviors through systematic observation; these questions help us understand the relation between behavior and context and help to provide a framework into which behaviors can be categorized. The four questions are displayed in Fig. 2.4.

1. Passive/noninteract
   sits
   stands
   lies
   eats
   watches
   waits turn
   reads/writes

2. Passive/interact
   talks to adult
   talked to by adult
   talks to peer
   talked to by peer
   gives comfort
   receives comfort
   grooms
   is groomed
   dresses
   is dressed
   offers object
   receives object
   refuses object

3. Aggression
   takes
   takes from
   kicks
   kicked
   swears
   sworn at

4. Distress
   cries

5. Football
   runs with ball
   runs without ball
   stands with ball
   watches in game
   gets attention
   catches
   tackles
   touches/tags
   throws

6. R & T
   play face
   plays/hits/kicks
   hits/kicks at
   play fights/wrestles (top)
   play fights/wrestles (bottom)
   carried
   carriers
   pouncers
   pounced
   pushes
   is pushed

7. Locomotion
   chases
   is chased
   walks
   skips
   hops
   dances
   balances
   climbs
   swings
   pushes on swing
   runs
   walks, following group or individual
   jumps

8. Games
   jumps rope
   plays ball
   catches
   throws
   follows leader
   tags
   claps/sings

9. Object
   touches/explores
   throws
   holds

10. Utterances
    social rules/norm statements
    aversive language
    threats
    contentions

FIG. 2.3.   Ethogram of children's playground behavior.

Question 1:   How does it work? (Proximal causes)
Question 2:   How did it develop? (Ontogeny)
Question 3:   What is the function? (Fitness/consequence)
Question 4:   How did it evolve? (Phylogeny)

FIG. 2.4.   Ethologists' four questions.

The first question asks: How does it work? Answering this question involves describing behavior in terms of the immediate (or proximate) causes of the behavior. Whereas the immediate causes could be external to the organism (e.g., availability of a valued resource) or internal to the organism (e.g., hormonal), internal and external causes often work in concert. For example, hormonal and social events typically precipitate aggression.

In choosing to examine causes external to the organism, we should describe social and physical dimensions of the context. Additionally, however, we must consider the behavioral context in which behaviors are embedded. By behavioral context, I mean those behaviors that directly precede and follow the targeted behaviors of our focal children. For example, if we are concerned with children's conflicts, we should try to describe the behaviors preceding conflicts and those following conflicts. The antecedents suggest possible causes of conflict, whereas the consequences tell us something about possible functions of the behavior. For example, if children's conflicts are preceded by disagreement about possession of toys, we can assume that object disputes lead to aggression (see Smith & Connolly, 1980). Furthermore, if possession of the prized toys follows the aggressive acts, we can assume that the aggression was motivated by the desire to possess the toy.

Tinbergen's second question is: How did the behavior of the individual develop during the life time? This developmental, or ontological, question is particularly important to those of us interested in observing young children and adolescents. Childhood and adolescence are periods during which the organism undergoes rapid and dramatic change. The second question explicitly tells us to focus on comparing these change processes. We try to examine, through the second question, the way in which specific behaviors change across time. A clear example of such developmental change involves children's attachment relationships with their primary caregiver. We may, at time 1 (say during the toddler period) observe two children's attachment status. One may be secure, and the other may be insecure. We track these relationships across time by observing the extent to which these relationships with their primary caregivers predict their relationships with their peers during the preschool period. It may be that the secure attachment relationship results in a child being friendly and popular with peers, whereas the insecure relationship may predict more troubled peer relations, with this child being aggressive and unpopular.

The importance of such documentation can be illustrated most clearly when we address the third question: What is the function of the behavior? Function in the strict biological sense refers to the reproductive success of the target organism or kin, but we can also consider function in terms of beneficial consequence (Hinde, 1980). Thus, the third question can be answered by examining consequences of behavior. This issue is relevant to the second question to the extent that the same behavior may have very different functions at different developmental periods. For example, crying for infants may be used to keep an adult in close proximity. With adolescents, on the other hand, crying may be a more private act.

An important concern in answering this question is to document the functions of behaviors within specific developmental periods. This translates into our being concerned with the meaning or function of the behavior for the child in question; we should not assume that the meaning of a behavior for a child is the same as for an adult. Considering the consequences of target behaviors for children within a specific developmental phase as well as possible future consequences helps to sort these things out.

The fourth, and final, question is the phylogenetic question and is concerned with the evolutionary history of the behavior: How did the behavior evolve across the history of the species? Although this concern may be of limited concern to most of us studying children, it is important to keep in mind that behaviors have a place in evolutionary history.

By way of illustration, I apply these four questions to observations of a hypothetical kindergarten child, Adam, as he sits listening to his teacher reading *The Tale of Peter Rabbit*. After finishing a page, the teacher, without mentioning a specific child's name, looks directly at Adam and asks: "What will Peter do now?" Adam says, "Run," and then he smiles; the teacher returns the smile and says, "Very good, Adam." Thus, we can describe Adam's verbalization in terms of its antecedents: teacher asks him a question. The second developmental question allows us to put this verbalization in the context of a child who has learned the rules of teacher–child questioning routines. The third question, that of function, points us toward examining the consequence of behaviors. In this case Adam's correct response resulted in his displaying positive affect as well as in the teacher praising him. The fourth question can be answered in terms of the evolutionary history of affiliative gestures in primates.

The four questions help us frame our observations by asking that we document both antecedent and consequences of specific behaviors. Additionally, we should consider the specific behavior in the developmental history of the individual child. An important consequence in applying the four questions to our observational techniques is that we move away from observing isolated bits of behavior and move toward observing sequences of behavior. In this way, behaviors are placed in their behavioral contexts as well as their physical and social contexts. Only through such contextualization can we begin to understand the meaning and function of behavior for the children and adults that we observe. In the next section, I consider another approach to observing children that also embeds them in their context.

Ecological Psychology

Ecological psychologists, like ethologists, also stress the importance of studying children in their everyday habitat (Gump, 1989). Consequently, both theories are concerned with the ways in which behaviors are categorized. Rather than relying on

Step 1:   Specimen record
Step 2:   Behavior setting survey

FIG. 2.5.   Steps in ecological observations.

pre-existent categories of behaviors, both use induced category systems. Behaviors are put into the categories that seem meaningful for the participants.

Although there are similarities between ethologists and ecological psychologists, there is a very important difference in the way in which each conceptualizes the relation between individuals and their environments. Ecological psychologists are concerned with describing the environmental effects on participants. That is, they stress descriptions of the effects of the environment, independent of individual participants. This independent effect of the environment on behavior is known as the *behavior setting*. For example, when children enter a block area of a classroom they all play in similar ways. Ethologists conceptualize the environment and the organism as influencing each other. That is, individuals shape and are shaped by the environment; different types of children play differently with the blocks. This difference in the way in which each school of thought conceptualizes the environment is probably related to ethology's orientation toward evolutionary theory, which minimizes the extent to which one can dichotomize the individual from the environment (Hinde, 1980).

Ecological psychologists generally follow a two-step process in conducting observations. These processes are displayed in Fig. 2.5.

First, ecological psychologists begin their observational studies by preparing a *specimen record*. The specimen record is a narrative description of each participant's behavior in a specific situation. The observer tries to describe everything about the child as a goal-directed individual in the environment. I believe it is neither practical nor possible to describe everything, but observers can describe most of the theoretically

relevant behaviors of focal children. The following example of a 5-year-old boy, playing with Legos at home with his father, is illustrative.

> 11:05 a.m. Anna looks at her father, who is sitting on the couch reading the newspaper: "Wanna play Legos, Dad?" Dad says, "Sure" and puts down the paper and gets on the floor. Anna pushes a pile of Legos toward Dad and says, "Here. You can build the factory with the volcanoes."

> 11:06 a.m. Dad looks puzzled and says, "What factory?" Anna laughs and says, "The one where they make molten steel, silly!" Dad say "Oh, I forgot" and picks up a gray lego and fits a red one to it.

Specimen records are often analyzed in terms of structure involving particular people (Gump, 1989). In the previous example, we have two possible episode structures: Anna soliciting Dad into play, or establishing a joint understanding of a play theme. These themes can then be catalogued as occurring in specific settings, in this case, home. Observers would collect numerous samples of Anna and her dad playing in the home and aggregate them into a representative sample of those episodes.

At the next level of analysis, the *behavior setting survey*, these individual cases (and aggregated individual cases) are aggregated across people, but the individual contexts are kept separate. Hence, we may have numerous cases of fathers playing with children at home. Depending on theoretical orientation, it might be important to include fathers of different ages as well as from different cultures. The aim of these surveys is to detect regularities across people within situations. Thus, ecological psychologists aim to establish standing patterns of behavior. By extension, ecological psychologists aim to describe the various behavior settings that children in a specific community experience. A comprehensive behavior setting survey describes various behavior settings (in our case, father–child play at home) across a whole community for a specified period of time. Like the ethologist's ethogram, the behavior setting survey provides an inventory of behavior in specific situations for a specific community.

SUMMARY AND CONCLUSIONS

In this chapter I have described a general orientation toward observations: the outsiders' perspective. This orientation recognizes the importance of observing children in their everyday habitats. The outsider perspective was represented by ethology and ecological psychology. Whereas ecological psychologists stress the role of the environment, independent of the participants, the ethological approach stresses the transaction between the environment and the participants. That is, participants and environments do not exist independent of each other; they affect each other.

In this book I follow the ethological orientation that people and environments affect each other. Dichotomizing the world into people and situations is as simplistic as dichotomizing nature–nurture and learning–development. The inherently developmental orientation of ethology is particularly attractive to me. In short, our job as observers is to describe the dynamic processes that characterize children and adults interacting in different situations.

THINGS TO THINK ABOUT

1. What are some things that might limit or bias emic-oriented data?

_____

_____

_____

_____

_____

2. What are some limits to assigning meaning to etic-oriented data?

_____

_____

_____

_____

_____

3. How would you go about choosing a key informant in a university class?

_____

_____

_____

_____

_____

_____

_____

4. Generate an ethogram for a university lecture class.

_____

_____

_____

_____

_____

_____

5. What are some situations in which there are very well established standing patterns of behavior? What might be some factors that would change this?

_____

_____

_____

_____

_____

_____

_____

GLOSSARY

Behavior setting survey: Specimen records aggregated across individuals.
Give your example:

_____

_____

_____

_____

_____

Ecological psychology: The study of the influence of context on behavior.
Give your example:

_____

_____

_____

_____

_____

Emic perspective: Derived from phonemic wherein researchers are concerned
with meaning distinction based on function. This orientation is often taken by
interpretative researchers.
Give your example:

_____

_____

_____

_____

_____

Ethogram: An inventory of behaviors for a species in a specific context.
Give your example:

_____

_____

_____

_____

_____

Ethology: The biological study of behavior.
Give your example:

_____

_____

_____

_____

_____

Etic perspective: Derived from phonetic wherein researchers are concerned with classifying based on degree or amplitude. This orientation is often taken by empirical researchers.
Give your example:

_____

_____

_____

_____

_____

Ontogeny: The study of development within a species.
Give your example:

_____

_____

_____

_____

_____

Phoneme: The smallest meaning unit of language which makes a difference in meaning; e.g., **cars** contains two phonemes.
Give your example:

_____

_____

_____

_____

_____

Phylogeny: The study of the development across animal species.
Give your example:

_____

_____

_____

_____

_____

Qualitative research: Loosely defined as researchers following an emic perspective.
Give your example:

_____

_____

_____

_____

_____

Quantitative research: Loosely defined as research following an etic perspective.
Give your example:

_____

_____

_____

_____

_____

Specimen record: Narrative descriptions of a participant's behavior in a specific context constructed by ecological psychologists.
Give your example:

_____

_____

_____

_____

_____

3

Design and Specifications of Observational Methods and Research

As we begin to consider conducting an observational project, a plan is of crucial importance. Consequently, a fair amount of preplanning is necessary in order to avoid some common problems that often afflict observational methods and research: An ounce of prevention. . . . In this chapter, I discuss some basics to be considered when planning and designing an observational project. Some of these are general and applicable to most observational work, such as observer bias, and some are very specific to conducting observations with young children, such as specific concerns with studying the development of the child (see Martin & Bateson, 1993, for additional discussion).

Probably the most basic choice to be made is that between conducting observations in a naturalistic, field setting and conducting observations in an experimental laboratory setting. This choice point is addressed first. Next, I discuss observer bias. Third, I discuss replication as a means to check against unusual or aberrational findings.

THE LABORATORY OR THE FIELD?

Although many of the issues associated with choosing between laboratory or field work were generally addressed in Chapter 2, aspects of those choices bear restating to the extent that it is probably the most basic choice in the design of observational work.

Field work can be either naturalistic or experimental. Naturalistic field work involves the observer studying the natural occurrence of behavior at a particular site. Field studies can also be experimental, as in the case of field experiments, where natural settings are experimentally manipulated. Examples of this include Smith and Connolly's (1980) manipulation of preschool classroom variables and Pellegrini and Davis' (1993) manipulation of recess timing. Typically, the choice between the field and the laboratory is determined by the investigators' predilection toward causal or descriptive work. Such a choice should be rooted in the nature of the question asked. A number of useful sources further explicate these differences, such as Kerlinger (1973).

Following Cronbach's (1957) characterization of the two disciplines of psychology (i.e., descriptive and explanatory), naturalistic observation typically belongs to the descriptive group, whereas experimental or laboratory studies belong to the causal–explanatory group. Thus, if one's question is primarily descriptive, the choice of a naturalistic setting may be more appropriate. The implication of conducting observations according to each of these traditions is presented in Table 3.1.

One typically chooses to conduct laboratory or experimental field studies because of the lure of causal explanations between independent and dependent measures. Causality is established by the manipulation of relevant (independent) variables and the control (or holding constant) of others in order to explain some outcome (or dependent) variable. Thus, children may be observed in a laboratory playroom in order to examine the effects of a specific set of toys (i.e., the manipulated, independent measures) on social behavior or language (i.e., the dependent measures). In laboratory procedures, a number of important variables are controlled, such as the composition of the play group in terms of age, gender, and familiarity, and the length of the play period. These variables are controlled so that they do not have an influence on the dependent variable. Any variation between groups or between toys sets is assumed to be due to the effects of the manipulated independent variable(s). An experiment is said to be internally valid if the only factors affecting the dependent variable are those manipulated by the experimenter. The student interested in possible threats to the internal validity of experiments, or one's ability to make unfettered statements about the effects of independent variables on dependent variables, is referred to the classic work on the validity of experiments by Campbell and Stanley (1967).

Observational methods applied to the laboratory are, obviously, very useful in helping to answer the hypothetical questions just posed. The often-noted limitation of the experimental approach is that it informs researchers about what children, and other research participants, can do rather than what they actually do (McCall, 1977). In short, experiments may give us insight into the effect of an independent variable on a dependent variable in a very specific setting; that, however, may not represent the world actually inhabited by the research participants.

TABLE 3.1
Types of Research With Setting and Inference Implications

Tradition	Venue	Nature of Inferences From Data	
Type of Research		Inference	Implications
Experimental	Laboratory or field	Descriptive causal	
Naturalistic	Field	Age specific	Descriptive
		Longitudinal	Developmental causal

This level of explanation may be a very different one from the ways in which this dependent variable develops in children in real life, outside of the laboratory. Thus, if we are interested in understanding the ways in which children develop in their everyday world, it seems imperative that, initially at least, we spend considerable time observing them in those situations that they ordinarily inhabit. As noted in the previous chapter in the discussion of ethological methods, studying children in their natural worlds is important to our understanding of development to the extent that development is considered a transactional process between children and their environments. It follows that in order to fully understand development we should observe children in those environments in which behaviors develop.

A promising compromise to a forced choice between the experimental/laboratory approach and the descriptive/field approach is the field experiment. Field experiments attempt to manipulate and control variables in real-world settings. For example, Smith and Connolly (1980) constructed preschool environments with different social densities to measure the effect of this variable on children's social behavior. Also, the recess periods of children in preschool (Smith & Hagan, 1980) and elementary school (Pellegrini & Davis, 1993; Pellegrini, Huberty, & Jones, 1995) have been experimentally manipulated to determine the effect of confinement on recess behavior. In all cases, experimental control and manipulation was applied to children in real classrooms, thus making causal inferences about children in real-world settings possible.

DEVELOPMENTAL RESEARCH IN THE FIELD: LONGITUDINAL AND CROSS-SECTIONAL DESIGNS

A very important aspect of field studies is the descriptive data that they generate. Observational methods are an important and probably crucial part of this descriptive process. The descriptions that we render can be focused on one specific age period of children or adults. More broadly, we can focus on the developmental processes typifying a specific period or periods. Observational methods are very closely associated with both age specific and developmental research but they are most closely associated with the naturalistic study of child development, rather than age specific behavior (Applebaum & McCall, 1983).

Developmental research involves charting the *change processes across time*. Although the developmental approach involves studying the same children or adults across time, it is not concerned primarily with cross-age comparisons of different groups. Cross-age comparisons are often included in developmental research, but the prime concern is to describe the change processes and mechanisms associated with change across time. Longitudinal research designs are necessary to accomplish this goal.

In longitudinal designs the same individuals are studied across time. In this way we can chart the change processes in the same individuals as they develop, and we can make cross-age comparisons. Study of different individuals at different ages utilizes cross-sectional designs. An example of a cross-sectional design might involve 3-, 4-, and 5-year-olds and could include a study of the age-related change of their aggressive behavior. In longitudinal research researchers study the ways in which a specific phenomenon, such as aggression, changes in a specific group across time. We might start off with a group of 3-year-olds and follow them, describing aggressive behavior, until they are 5 years old.

As noted previously, longitudinal designs are necessary in order to study development. Indeed, McCall (1977) called longitudinal research the "life blood" of developmental psychology. The reasoning is straightforward enough: If one is interested in studying the change processes across time rather than differences between age groups, one must study the way in which a group of individuals changes across that time span. Like the marriage between naturalistic researchers and observational methods, so too a marriage exists between longitudinal research and observational methods.

Thus, longitudinal designs are a necessary component of doing developmental research, and they have the added benefit of allowing us to begin to make directional inferences about relations between sets of variables. Specifically, in longitudinal designs we have, by definition, variables in antecedent-consequence relations, such as, parent–child interaction patterns at time 1 and sociometric status at time 2. Such antecedent-consequence relations are necessary but not sufficient for making causal inferences. With the advent of various path analytic and structural equation data analysis procedures, we can begin to make causal inferences about longitudinal data (see the special issue of *Child Development, 58,* edited by Connell and Tanaka, 1987, on structural modeling).

I will flesh out this example a bit more to demonstrate this important point of how longitudinal designs can be used to proffer causal explanations. In order to make causal explanations, antecedent-consequence relations are necessary but not sufficient. If we want to make an inference about the effects of parenting styles on children's acceptance by their peers, we must have some measure of parenting that precedes our measure of peer acceptance: parenting (x) → peer acceptance (y). This temporal relation allows us to make predictive statements, such that x predicts y. In order to move from predictions to causal explanation we must try to do what experimenters do—we must control or eliminate the effects of extraneous variables on dependent measures while measuring the effects of the independent variables. Certain statistical procedures, such as partial correlations and hierarchical regression techniques, allow us to control the effects of variables other than parenting strategies that might affect children's peer acceptance, such as socioeconomic status and the child's physical attractiveness. Controlling alternative sources of variance is not adequate, however, to proffer a causal explanation. To make a causal argument we must do one of two things: experimentally manipulate independent variables (in this case parenting styles) or use sophisticated path analytical techniques (like LISREL) or structural equation models that test a specific theory.

To summarize this section, those of us wishing to observe children in the field can do so by describing a specific group at a specific age. Alternatively, we can describe the change processes in a specific group as the group develops across time. This latter approach has the added benefit of allowing us to make predictive interferences about the relations between variables. The relative assets and deficits of cross-sectional and longitudinal designs are summarized in Table 3.2.

TABLE 3.2
Assets and Deficits of Cross-Sectional and Longitudinal Designs

Design	Assets	Deficits
Cross-sectional	Short term	No change/process measures
	Cross-age comparisons	Measures are contemporaneous
Longitudinal	Measures change/process	Costly and long term
	Antecedent-consequence relationship	

In the next section, we begin to consider some very specific issues in planning observational research.

OBSERVER BIAS

Observer bias should be a concern to all researchers (see Martin & Bateson, 1993, for an additional discussion). By observer bias I mean the expectations and knowledge observers have about participants that may influence the objectivity of their observations per se or the ways in which they treat participants and data derived from observations. Observer bias applied to experimental situations results when observers know, for example, to which groups (e.g., treatment or control group) participants have been assigned. Such knowledge may influence results to the extent that experimenters may provide subtle cues to the children about the adequacy or inadequacy of their behavior. For example, an experimenter's smile or

subtle nod may encourage a child to continue responding in a specific way whereas a frown or look of surprise from an observer may result in a behavior, being terminated by the participant. Thus, observers' biases affect their behavior which, in turn, affects the behavior of the participants.

I stress that these biases probably operate subconsciously on the observer. Most biased observers are not being dishonest; they are simply emitting behavior that reflects their anticipations. One very well established and simple way of alleviating this type of bias is to assure that observers are *blind* to hypotheses, group assignment, or both. *Double blind* procedures involve neither the experimenter/observer nor the participant knowing the treatment the latter has received.

A related problem that afflicts observations in both the laboratory and the field involves bias among observers who record and score, or code, behavioral data. This sort of bias, too, can arise from knowledge of hypotheses or group assignment. For example, behaviorally similar responses from children in different groups, such as an experimental and a control group, may be coded differently by a biased coder. Observers may be more likely to code a child's behavior in specific ways if they knew the child was in an experimental or a control group. Such bias can also affect nonexperimental research designs. If an observer knows the research hypothesis, say that boys' play is rougher than girls', then the observer may be biased toward describing boys' and girls' behavior in ways that are consistent with the hypothesis.

Bias often results from observers' awareness of participants' status on other measures. This knowledge may influence the ways in which observers record and code behavior. For example, if one researcher collects sociometric and behavioral data on the same children, the knowledge of the children's sociometric status may influence the ways in which ambiguous behavior is coded. If the researcher knows that a specific child has been frequently nominated as being "disliked" and "nasty" by peers, the observer may more readily code an ambiguous behavioral act, such as rough-and-tumble play, as aggressive for that child. Another child, receiving numerous "liked" and "kind" nominations, may have exhibited similarly ambiguous behavior but, because of observer bias, that behavior is coded as rough play, not aggression. In other words, the observer's coding of behavior is being influenced by knowledge of children's reputations.

The issue of bias is a very important one to the extent that such biases have real effects on children and the ways in which observers categorize their behaviors. The children's play literature has some very interesting cases where very well recognized effects of play on dimensions of children's creativity were seemingly due to bias. In three very frequently cited studies (Dansky & Silverman, 1973, 1975; Sylva, Bruner, & Genova, 1976), the researchers suggested that forms of play with objects facilitated creative object use and problem solving. None of these studies, however, controlled for observer bias. That is, experimenters interacting with children in the experimental and testing conditions and observers coding children's responses knew the specific hypotheses and children's group assignment. This knowledge probably affected the ways in which they interacted with the children in the training and testing situations as well as the ways in which they coded children's responses. In subsequent studies where observer bias was controlled, the Dansky and Silverman (1973, 1975) studies were not replicated by Smith and Whitney (1987); nor were the

Sylva et al. (1976) results replicated by Simon and Smith (1983) or Vandenberg (1980). It is incumbent on observers to address the issue of bias. Using blind procedures, observers should check their undue influence on participants' behavior.

REPLICATION

One way in which to guard against the acceptance of unreliable empirical findings is through *replication*. One way to define replication is, generally, where an attempt is made to attain the same results using the same measures with similar participants in similar situations. The null hypothesis is rejected (that is, we can say that there are reliable difference between groups) only when similar results are obtained in both groups. Remember the case of cold fusion where researchers could not replicate the original findings; the original findings supporting cold fusion were consequently disregarded.

Literal replication can be accomplished within a research team or across different research teams. Within one research team, a replication sample design can be utilized such that two parallel groups, rather than single groups, are studied for each question. Results are accepted by the researcher if they are similar across the two samples. Smith and Pellegrini have utilized replication samples in studying the effects of play deprivation on preschool children's motor behavior outdoors (Smith & Hagan, 1980; Pellegrini et al., 1995) and the effects of various classroom ecological arrangements on children's and teachers' behavior (Smith & Connolly, 1980). In these cases, two separate groups of children were assigned to different treatment and comparison groups. Graphically, the research design might look like that presented in Fig. 3.1. Results are accepted, that is, replicated across samples, if the treatment versus comparison difference exist in both Group 1 and Group 2.

Although exact or literal replication is very difficult, an attempt can be made by one group of researchers to reproduce results of another group under reasonably similar circumstances (Lykken, 1970; Martin & Bateson, 1993). In this vein, researchers attempt to draw a sample and reconstruct the situation and procedures in ways that are similar to the study they are trying to replicate. The researcher then compares the results to those of the original study. This sort of replication was conducted by Simon and Smith (1983) and Smith and Whitney (1987) discussed in the section on observer bias.

Bronfenbrenner's (1979) notion of ecological validity of experimental results is relevant here. Although not treated as replication per se, ecological validity has one

	Group 1	Group 2
Treatment 1		
Treatment 2		
Comparison		

FIG. 3.1   Replication sample design.

research team comparing the results of an experiment with naturalistic results. For example, children could be observed interacting with peers and toys in their preschool classrooms. Then the same or similar children would be observed playing in similar social groupings with similar toys in an experimental analogue to that classroom. The similarity or replication of the results across the two settings determines the ecological validity of the experiment (see Pellegrini & Perlmutter, 1989).

Yet another form of replication, labeled *constructive replication* by Martin and Bateson (1993), involves very different samples and methods converging with similar results. For example, in studies of relations between preschool children's oral language and early literacy, Dickinson and Moreton (1991) and Pellegrini and Galda (1991) studied preschool children in the northeastern and southeastern U.S., respectively, in very different classrooms and using different measures of language and literacy. Despite these differences, their results converged on the finding that specific types of language and symbolic play predicted early literacy. Thus, similar results were obtained by different groups examining a similar question in different ways.

Replication is a conservative approach to accepting research findings. It is also a safeguard against accepting empirical findings prematurely. Indeed, replication should be instituted as a component of our research models and designs. This becomes a particularly important issue when we consider that so much of our child study data have policy implications. Think of the folly involved, not to mention the effects on the lives of children and their families and resources wasted, when we design specific projects, such as infant day programs or whole language reading curricula, based on limited research bases. Replication should be a hallmark by which we accept or fail to accept a finding. It is part of the scientific enterprise. Replication should be put, again, into the foreground of observational research; we have our own lessons, as in the cases of the nonreplication of the previously presented play findings, which point to its importance.

SUMMARY AND CONCLUSIONS

In this chapter, I have pointed out some particular issues that I see as important in designing any observational work. As stressed in earlier chapters, a fair amount of preplanning is necessary. Some of the more basic issues to be resolved involve observer bias, which probably requires using multiple observers, and issues of interdependence. If these issues are not considered prior to the actual observations, the data generated will be of limited use. These problems can be particularly insidious because they all lend themselves toward confirming preexisting conceptions of what we think we will find. Specifically, bias generally operates to confirm our hypotheses, whether they are stated as such or not. To my mind, research is conducted to find something out, not merely to reinforce what we already think we know. We, as researchers, students, and teachers should keep an open mind and objectively seek answers to our questions, even when the answers are other than those we want to hear.

SOME THINGS TO THINK ABOUT

1. What are some children's traits that you consider continuous? (Hint: Height is continuous.)

_____

_____

_____

_____

_____

_____

_____

2. What are some children's traits that are discontinuous? (Hint: The Piagetian concept of intelligence is discontinuous.)

_____

_____

_____

_____

_____

_____

_____

3. What are some ways in which teachers and other practitioners can guard against bias in observations of their students?

_____

_____

_____

_____

_____

_____

_____

_____

4. Select children from more than one classroom defined by their teachers as "very smart" and "not so smart." Next, videotape each child while the child is engaged in some cognitive task, such as doing a puzzle or writing. Show the videos of the children to the teachers whose classrooms these children *are not* in. Tell some teachers that specified children are smart and not so smart; you, as the researcher should mislabel some children and accurately label some children for the teachers viewing the videos. Have the teachers, individually, tell you why they think the smart kids are smart and the not-so-smart kids are that way. Then, assemble teachers in a group and compare their descriptions of the same children whom you initially labeled as smart and not so smart. Do we sometimes make inferences about behavior based on our attributions?

_____

_____

_____

_____

_____

_____

_____

GLOSSARY

Antecedent–consequence relations: When two variables are ordered such that one precedes the other. For example, a child's infant daycare experience is antecedent to its later peer popularity.
Give your example:

_____

_____

_____

_____

_____

Bias: When observers, experimenters, or subjects know the hypotheses of the research, which group the subjects belong to, or have additional information that results in differential treatment.
Give your example:

_____

_____

_____

_____

Blind and double blind: Blind refers to situations in which experimenters or observers are not aware of the research hypotheses. Double blind refers to situations in which neither the experimenters/observers nor the participants are aware of the hypotheses. These procedures are used to minimize bias.
Give your example:

_____

_____

_____

_____

Control: Control in experiments refers to the procedure of minimizing the influence of certain factors on experimental results. For example, the influence of the intelligence of children on experimental results can be controlled by randomly assigning children to experimental and control groups. Variables of interest are manipulated.

Give your example:

_____

_____

_____

_____

Cross-sectional research: Research that examines age-related phenomena by studying different children from each of the relevant age groups.

Contrast with *longitudinal*:

_____

_____

_____

_____

Dependent variable: In experiments, this is the variable that is affected by the independent variable. For example, play is the dependent variable in an experiment in which we are examining the effect of toys on play.

Give your example:

_____

_____

Development, continuous: When a construct, like aggression, is stable across the developmental time of an individual. For example, aggression would be continuous development if it were stable in an individual across time.

Give your example:

Development, discontinuous: When a construct, like perspective-taking, changes across developmental time. For example, perspective taking would be discontinuous if at point 1 a child had low-level perspective taking and at point 2 had a higher level.

Give your example:

Field: Refers to the real world where behaviors actually occur. For example, a field might be a classroom or a home environment.

Contrast with *laboratory*:

Independent variable: In experiments, this is the variable that is manipulated and has an effect on the dependent variable. For example, in an experiment looking at the effect of gender on play behavior, the independent would be gender.

Give your example:

Laboratory: This is the venue for experimental research, often an experimental playroom or classroom.

Contrast with *field*:

Longitudinal: This form of research is concerned with describing the process of change in the same children as they develop across time.

Contrast with *cross-sectional*:

_____

_____

Manipulation: In experiments, variables of interest are changed to determine their effect. For example, we could manipulate different toys to see their effect on children's play. Other variables should be controlled.
    Give your example:

_____

_____

_____

_____

Replication: This refers to the degree to which the same results can be obtained in more than one group.
    Give your example:

_____

_____

_____

_____

4

Initial Considerations

TAKING THE FIRST STEPS INTO THE FIELD

In this chapter, I discuss the initial stages involved in conducting observational research. Although we are typically motivated to undertake an observational study for practical or scientific reasons, the specifics of the observational process per se remain vague until we actually enter the field that we are planning to study. No matter how well formulated our ideas may be, those ideas must interface with the specific situations that we observe.

Oftentimes, as many observers will tell, the specific contingencies of observational sites necessitate reconsideration, sometimes major, of original plans. For example, we may find out by initial observations that specific room arrangements preclude the use of video equipment. More basically, we may find out that what it is we are interested in observing does not occur with any regularity in the situations in which we thought it would occur. Taking an example from my own work, I found only after a substantial period of observations that aggression on the playground of a particular school was virtually nonexistent. Although this was very good news for children, parents, teachers, and school administrators, it left me without a study site. A recent vigorous campaign at the school to eliminate fighting (through the use of more playground supervisors, parent newsletter announcements, and strict enforcement of rules) had been successful; my initial observations certainly supported this conclusion!

In many if not most cases, however, we conduct observations in someone else's territory. For example, we may observe in someone's classroom or in a doctor's waiting room. In these cases, observers must come to terms with key or infrastructural personnel occupying the observational site. Becoming familiar with the infrastructural personnel is an important early phase in the early phase of field work; for this reason I address it first. Then I discuss the ways in which initial observations are useful in question formulation, behavioral category definition and measurement, and habituation of subjects to observers' presence.

Two other important aspects of the observational plan also require preplanning: deciding when to observe and deciding how much to observe. Specifically, we discuss when data should be collected. The time of the day and the day of the week have obvious and important implications for the sorts of data collected. Mother–child interactions collected on Monday mornings before school and work look very different from observations of the same folk on Saturday morning. Lastly, the amount of data that should be collected is discussed. The amount of data collected, both on individual cases and across individuals, has important implication for the representativeness of our data. Deciding when and how much to observe, then, are sampling issues of sorts. That is, we are deciding what part of the day is best to observe those things that we are interested in observing. How much data are representative of the phenomena of interest? What amount is required to make reasonable inferences?

The precautions outlined in this chapter should be considered before a researcher begins a project. That is not to say that one will not have to make adjustments during the actual data collection portion of the work, of course; the precautions outlined in this chapter represent some of the more common problems that can be anticipated.

BECOMING FAMILIAR WITH INFRASTRUCTURAL PERSONNEL

Researchers entering a site to conduct observations are guests at that site. As guests, their status is always tenuous but is particularly tenuous at the start of the project. One version of this tenuous arrangement has been labeled "mutually voluntary and negotiated entree" by Schatzman and Strauss (cited in Corsaro, 1981). Key personnel grant permission to the researcher to conduct business at the site; this permission can be revoked at any point thereafter. Thus, familiarity with key personnel at the observational site is very important. In some cases they are "gatekeepers," to use Corsaro's (1981) apt term, because they exercise control over access to the site. Teachers, administrators, and often custodians are gatekeepers in schools.

In addition to the issue of initial and continued access to the site, this phase of the observation is important for ethical and practical reasons. Some useful hints for initial encounters with infrastructure personnel are displayed in Fig. 4.1.

Ethically, many researchers, but particularly ethnographers such as Hymes and Corsaro, argue that the research enterprise should be a collaborative venture between participants and researchers. This stance, as Hymes (1980) noted most forcefully, can democratize the research process to the extent that interpretations of both participants and researchers are given equal consideration in the planning and interpretation of the project. Indeed, many observers who have conducted research in institutions such as schools, communities, and hospitals often meet initial reluc-

1. Schedule meetings as needed
2. Present versions of tentative plans
3. Be democratic/seek input
4. Have a collegial relationship
5. Co-authorship
6. Material rewards

FIG. 4.1.   Interacting with infrastructure personnel.

tance. This reluctance is often the result of previous experience with researchers who have come into the site, imposed their way of looking at the site on the situation (often without much of a preobservation phase), collected their data, and left without further contact.

Such exploitation of participants by researchers can be illustrated with a very simple and common curiosity that is typically ignored by researchers. While negotiating entrance to the research site, the researcher, of course, assures participants that they will share the data and final reports. Frequently, however, researchers forget their obligations after they have data in hand and have left the site. Firsthand, I myself have experienced this at the hands of one sort of behavioral observer: newspaper reporters. Reporters sometimes call me to get information on a story they are writing. I give information contingent on their agreeing to clear with me the ways in which that information is used, before publication. Unfortunately this rarely happens. Not only do I resent being misled, but I feel exploited. Such exploitation is indeed unethical. Thus, we as researchers should treat others as we want to be treated. Simple enough.

Open communication between observers and infrastructure personnel also has practical advantages. Certainly exploitative actions of the sort outlined previously will not result in the particular researcher, or indeed other researchers, being invited back. Thus, continued access to a data site is at stake. Additionally, getting to know the key people at the site enables the researcher to gain a valued data source. At one level, specific individuals can serve a key informant role. As the meaning and function of specific aspects of the situation being observed may be tactic, in order to unravel the meaning a key informant may be necessary. Key personnel can also serve as sounding boards for ideas. For example, they may provide insight into interpretation of certain events. At another level, insiders can provide valuable logistical information. For example, if a researcher is interested in using a specific type of recording device, teachers may be very helpful in suggesting specific locations where recorders can be placed.

Perhaps the best way to proceed with this phase of the observation is first to present the plan of the research to the key infrastructural personnel. It has been my experience that researchers conducting field research should have variations of their research plan, ranging from the ideal plan (from the researcher's perspective) to the bare essential plan. Researchers should first prepare an explicit statement of the question that they are interested in studying. Next, they should present various versions of the plan (from the ideal to the bare essentials) to the group. Researchers should remain tentative, remembering their status as guests, not wanting to be intrusive. Preschool, primary, and middle school teachers and the parents of these children are usually very eager to please. Indeed, they typically take on difficult and cumbersome tasks and scheduling regimens if they feel as though they have a stake in the project.

By having a stake I mean that they should be given an opportunity to provide input at various points in the project, such as planning the observations and in some cases the interpretation of the results. For this reason, researchers should keep in contact with personnel to make sure that things are running smoothly. Too many meetings and communications can be a nuisance in the busy lives of our hosts; we must maintain a good balance here.

Different degrees of participation in the research can also be rewarded differentially. In the field of education, it is becoming quite common for university researchers to enter into collaborative relationships with researchers at field sites. In these cases, joint authorship of papers is in order. This strategy, recommended by Heath (1983, 1985) and Hymes (1980) a number of years ago, has taken hold in the field of early literacy research in school settings (e.g., Heath, 1985).

Other types of rewards can be offered for participation in research. It is common, for example, for researchers to build financial or material compensation (e.g., books and computers for the school) into their proposals for funded research.

The last suggestion is an obvious one and that is to treat people well and with respect. Do what you promise to do. By following these simple rules, a researcher will not only maintain a good relationship with the personnel at the site but will probably also collect better data and have more valid interpretations of the data. In short, the lesson of this chapter, presented in advance, is do not be in a hurry to begin formal data collection. Plan for a specific period of preliminary observation; the time and effort expended in this phase will pay high dividends later. Some of the specifics of this preplanning were outlined in Chapter 3, and more information is presented in Chapter 6.

THE NATURE OF THE QUESTION

Any observation, indeed any research, should be motivated by a specific question or series of questions that the researcher is interested in answering. The questions may be of scientific interest, such as charting the development of children's ability to read, or of practical interest, such as developing an effective method for teaching young children to read. By the nature of the examples given, it should be clear that the distinction between basic and applied research is in some cases artificial and in others very blurred. In all cases, our aim is to understand the ways in which children and adults carry on their everyday lives. Thus, I use the term *research* to include both basic and applied dimensions of the enterprise by which we come to know about phenomena.

Generally, the questions that motivate our research are, at first, pretty global. For example, we may be interested in studying the occurrence of aggression on the playground or children's use of oral language in their preschool and primary school classrooms. Preliminary observations should be conducted in the situation in which we think they occur. Further, we should observe the phenomena according to our current conceptualizations. Obviously, our conceptualization of the research question, the methods we plan on using, and the specific behavioral and verbal categories that we plan on using should all be based on a thorough reading of the research literature. That is the starting point.

So, taking the oral language example, we might start observing children in specified classrooms across the school day. These preliminary observations should help us to more explicitly formulate our questions regarding the oral language of specific classrooms. We may find that in one classroom there is lots of oral language and that very different types of language are used when children talk with their friends compared to when they talk with peers who are not friends. In another classroom we may find that children's oral language is limited to answering teachers' questions. Thus, at one level, we have reformulated our question to consider three types of discourse participants (i.e., teachers, friends, and nonfriend peers).

Correspondingly, preliminary observations may enable us to develop specific hypotheses about the ways in which language is used in specific situations. We may or may not then choose to make specific predictions about the ways in which specific types of oral language are used in different situations.

Thus, the preliminary observation period enables the observer to specify more exactly the nature of the question guiding the research. Without such an entry period, the observer is assuming that what they have read about other research projects is all they need to know to study their specific situation. This is probably not the case. The orientations of those researchers whose reports we have read may be very different from ours. That we are motivated by different concerns necessitates that we formulate our questions specifically in situations that are most meaningful to us.

A useful way to organize our preliminary observational notes was suggested by Corsaro (1981). In his initial observations in a preschool classroom Corsaro organized the notes he took on the situation into field notes (FN), personal notes (PN), methodological notes (MN), and theoretical notes (TN). Generally, FN are behavioral recordings of the participants and the their locations. With preliminary observation, this may involve the researcher writing descriptions of the situation after he or she leaves the field; to record in the field may be too obtrusive. MN notes include comments on logistics, such as the ability to use a specific type of equipment or coding scheme. PN give insight the observer's personal reaction to specific situations and people, for example, noting that one of the teachers may be feeling left out of the research process. Lastly, TN are larger considerations relating to the nature of the question being posed or the (re)formulation of a specific hypotheses.

Although the researcher may initially think it unnecessary to record observational phenomena that occur repeatedly and are quite obvious, records of all relevant phenomena should be made. It is often the case that what seems obvious and unlikely to be forgotten is often forgotten after hours of observation. In short, records should be kept of what one considers important, no matter how obvious. Organizing initial observations into relevant categories, such as those suggested by Corsaro, seems very sensible. It allows the observer to consider the multitudinous layers of information into separate categories. This level of organization should make the final observation plan more organized and debugged.

MUTUAL HABITATION: GETTING USED TO EACH OTHER

Conducting systematic observations can be obtrusive. By this I mean that when we, as observers, decide to examine someone closely for a period of time we inevitably have an effect on them. If we are interested in describing the natural lives of our participants, it is imperative that we minimize any obtrusion. The period of initial observation is crucial in this regard to the extent that it gets participants and observers used to each other. The extent that they take each other's presence for granted is, in turn, related to the unobtrusiveness of the observational procedure. Generally, participants habituate to obtrusion as time progresses. Of course, the more obtrusive the observer or procedure, the longer the time needed for habituation.

Probably the least obtrusive is the participant observer, especially if he or she is a natural part of the observational setting, such as a teacher who is a participant observer in his or her own classroom. In this case, the observer is part of the natural scene and thus is minimally obtrusive. What may be obtrusive in this situation, however, is the procedure associated with the observation. For example, the participant observer may use recording devices, such as video cameras or portable radio microphones, or note-taking strategies to which the subjects must habituate.

In the case of a researcher wishing to take a participant observer role, though not one corresponding with actually being employed in the setting, it makes most sense to be at the setting when the focal subjects first enter. For example, if we are interested in studying children in schools, observers should be situated in the classroom on the morning of the very first day of class. In this way participants associate the observer with the normal setting.

Participant observers should decide in advance the stance they wish to take as participants. Do they want to be treated as if they were children (see Corsaro, 1981)? Do they want to be treated as teachers' aids? Because the specific details of the participant observer approach are not discussed in great detail, the interested reader is referred to Corsaro (1981), Fine and Sandstrom (1988), and Patton (1990). Suffice it to say that participant observers want to be considered as part of the natural setting; thus, they should attend when the participants attend. Correspondingly, introduction of any sort of recording devices should be put off until the observer thinks participants have accepted him or her in the appropriate role.

The strategy with nonparticipant observers is very different. By nonparticipant observer, I mean an observer who wants to maintain objective distance from those being observed. In the best of all possible worlds, the nonparticipant observer wishes to be a fly on the wall of the research setting. Thus, these researchers try to conceal themselves behind blinds or one-way viewing screens or in inconspicuous locations within a research setting. In some cases, to minimize the effects of their presence, researchers leave tape recorders in room to collect language data (see Dunn, 1982, for an interesting example of this approach).

It has been my direct experience that researchers must spend a fair amount of preliminary time in the setting so that participants get used to them and their procedures. By way of illustration, in one project (see Pellegrini & Galda, 1991) my colleagues and I had preschool children wearing radio microphones in vests so that we could record their oral language as they played in their classroom. We also video-recorded them from an adjacent observation room through a one-way viewing screen. When children put on the vest we asked them to say their names so that we could have a voice print when we coded the data so that we would be able to distinguish the voice of the focal child from others. Initially children performed for the microphone to the extent that they used exaggerated and loud voices. After numerous observations per child, however, we knew that they were getting used

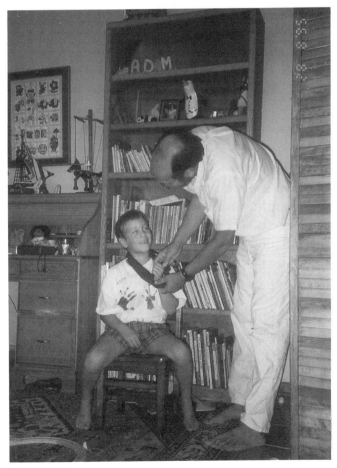

to them: Some youngsters, while huddled in a corner, would use "nasty" language. (Dunn, 1993, also mentioned this as a criterion for children being unaware that they are being observed.) I don't think they would have used such language had they been conscious of being recorded. That is not to say that children habituate totally to such devices; I mean that the devices become less obtrusive with time.

Similar time and caution is needed when observing from behind blinds. In some cases these blinds may be permeable. Another personal example: Both of my children, as preschoolers, attended the UGA preschool. Each classroom has adjoining observational rooms and one-way screens through which children can be observed. It was my habit, as part of my picking-up-children routine and because I am a compulsive child-watcher, to drop into the observational room to see what they were doing. On numerous occasions, a child in the classroom looked directly at me through the screen and then said, "Adam/Anna. Your Dad's here."

In short, we as observers must take time to have participants get used to our presence. Again, I am not suggesting that participants totally habituate to us. What I am suggesting is that with time they act in a way that approaches the way they would act if we were not there. The preliminary observation period, thus, is indispensable in this process. Data collected before a reasonable habituation period are questionable at best. They do little to advance our understanding of the phenomena under consideration. In the fields of developmental psychology and education this type of data becomes part of what Bronfenbrenner (1979) described as those collected for as brief a period as possible under strange conditions. This is, at best, a questionable enterprise.

WHEN TO OBSERVE?

The design issues discussed in the next two sections of this chapter (i.e., when to observe and how much to observe) are very basic yet must be given clear consideration and forethought. As noted in earlier in this chapter, some preliminary observations may be necessary to determine the time that specific behaviors can best be observed. We simply cannot observe all participants all the time. We must determine the best times for observing target behaviors and then determine the appropriate amount of data to be collected. These issues are clearly sampling issues and are related to the representativeness of our data.

Although some of us jokingly respond to students' queries about time and frequency of observations with "As often and for as long as possible," there is some value in this advice. Regarding when to observe, laboratory researchers generally have eliminated this problem by observing participants during the whole experimental period. There are variations on this procedure. One such exception is where aspects of the observational period are sampled. For example, in one study of parent–child interaction we (Pellegrini, Brody, & Sigel, 1985) observed parents reading books to their children. The whole session was videorecorded, but only 5 minutes were coded, the first and last 2 minutes and the middle 1 minute. I discuss the nature of sampling in later in this chapter; suffice it to say that one should have good reasons for sampling specific intervals. In other words, observers' sampling choices should be guided by some theory: What do we think the sample intervals represent? In the book reading example, we decided that most teaching probably went on at the beginning and end; thus, we sampled longer from those points.

A related issue for both experimenters and field researchers is the length of the specific observations periods. This issue overlaps with issues concerning how much to observe. The variation in the durations of the observation periods in various laboratory and field observations is striking. Some laboratory researchers observe children and parents for a 10- to 15-minute period, whereas others conduct more frequent and longer observations. Similarly, some field observations involve single observations, say in the home, around one event like book reading. Others, most notably Haight and Miller (1992) conduct long (i.e., approximately 5 hours) and repeated observations.

The issue of when to observe is related to the representativeness of the observations. That is, do the observations capture what we want them to capture. For the experimentalist, representativeness can probably be maximized by conducting multiple observations of participants in each context of interest; these multiple observations, then, should be aggregated so that there is one score per context. For example, if we observe children playing with blocks twice and with dolls twice, the two blocks observations should be aggregated into one score as should the two doll scores. Repeated observations and aggregation have the effects of minimizing random variability and, consequently, error in our data analyses. In short, laboratory observers should choose a time interval based on some theory; then they should observe a phenomenon on more than one occasion and aggregate across occasions. Continuing with the parent–child book reading example, length of individual observations periods could be based on the average time parents spend reading a book to their children at home.

The issue of when to observe becomes more complicated for the field observer. The first concern is to determine when during the day the phenomenon of interest usually occurs. For example, we may be interested in observing the ways in which young children encounter mathematics at home, yet initially we have no idea when this happens or with whom. In a later chapter I discuss various ways of addressing the issue of inventorying children's actions throughout their day with spot sampling and diary techniques, but the when to observe issue can and probably should be addressed in the preliminary stage of the observation. Martin and Bateson (1993) offered specific strategies that may be helpful in answering the when to observe question during the preliminary stage. These strategies are displayed in Fig. 4.2.

First, observers could continuously observe in a specific context such as a home by following a focal child for a full 24 hours. This tack is not very practical for most of us to the extent that numerous observers are probably necessary and it would most likely meet opposition from participants. By way of compromise, we can sample the 24-hour period by making separate observations during morning,

1. Continuous for 24 hours
2. Sample different parts of the day
3. Observe only one part of the day

FIG. 4.2.   When to observe?

afternoon, and evening sessions. This sampling of different times should inform the observer as to the time and place that the phenomenon of interest occurs.

Once we know when the phenomenon of interest occurs we can then concentrate on observing during those periods. If more than one period is relevant, such as morning and evening, then the observer must decide after extensive observation the extent to which data from each of those periods are similar or dissimilar; if similar, observations can be conducted at either place and then aggregated. If they are not similar then observations should be collected systematically at each and not aggregated.

The second recommendation is to observe systematically across different parts of the day and then to aggregate these observations (Martin & Bateson, 1993). This approach allows the observer to construct a reasonable picture across the whole day. Obvious limitations to this approach are logistical; for example, will participants tolerate observers in their presence at all times of the day and night? From the observer's perspective, scheduling observations at different times is both time consuming and difficult.

The third approach ignores the problem and observes only at one time of the day, say dinner time (Martin & Bateson, 1993). We might label this the strategy of maximum convenience, but it is limited to the extent that results can only be

generalized to that part of the day. More troublesome, however, is the real possibility that the phenomenon of interest may not be occurring at that time or if it does occur, it may take a different form in other parts of the day.

If the observer chooses limited time periods within each day to conduct observations, that is, strategies 2 and 3, some guidance is needed as to the length of time to observe. Wachs (1985) suggested a minimum of 1½ hours per observation for field observations. Numerous observations should then be conducted, and they should then be aggregated at the appropriate interval, such as mornings only or across the whole day.

HOW MUCH TO OBSERVE?

How much observational data are necessary? This issue relates to the number of participants in the study, the number of observations for each participant, and the duration of those observations. Despite this variety, there is (at one level) a rather simple answer to this question, like the answer to the when to observe question: as much as possible. There is one reason behind the similar answers to the two questions: Larger samples, whether they be samples of participants or samples of different times of day, more closely represent that population of people or universe of behaviors to which we hope to generalize.

If, on the other hand, we are only interested in studying a small group and not making inferences about a population, a larger sample of observations, compared to a smaller sample of observations, more closely approximates the universe of the behaviors of those specific participants. In short, one reason for "more being better" is that large samples are usually more representative of the population than are smaller samples.

More is also better in terms of statistical analyses of observational data. Larger samples of participants and larger numbers of observations usually result in less sampling error and error variance, where sampling error is the degree of uncertainty about a sample; as the sample increases, error decreases (Suen & Ary, 1989). Sampling error may be particularly problematic in cases of a heterogeneous or very diverse sample compared to homogeneous sample, which has very similar participants (Suen & Ary, 1989). Because homogeneous samples have fewer differences, there will be less error; therefore, we can get away with smaller samples.

SUMMARY AND CONCLUSIONS

In this chapter, I have discussed the importance of preliminary observations. This phase of the observational process is indispensable. It is indispensable because without it, we would probably have limited access to data collection sites; we would ask poor questions, collect unreliable and invalid data, and then go on to proffer even more off-base explanations. Thus, the scientific integrity of our work depends on careful preliminary observations. Correspondingly, preliminary observations allow us to enter into a dialogue with our participants. Not only is this a basically democratic act, but it also helps us make more informed decisions.

In this chapter I have pointed out some particular issues that I see as important in implementing any observational work. Based on preliminary observations we should have some idea as to when to observe. The issue of amount of observation time, or how much to observe, is more closely related to issues of sampling and reliability, presented in later chapters. Again, preplanning is necessary. If we ignore preplanning, the quality of the data collected suffer. For example, when we have a limited number of observations of a group or we observe them only at a few specified time, our data are limited. The time of our observations, like the categories themselves, should clearly relate to the questions we have in mind.

THINGS TO THINK ABOUT

1. Identify the key infrastructure personnel in a school, in a pediatrics practice, and at a summer camp.

_____

_____

_____

_____

_____

_____

1a. How could you gain access to that setting and those people?

_____

_____

_____

_____

_____

_____

1b. What do you have to offer them?

_____

_____

_____

_____

_____

_____

_____

1c. What can you learn from each of them?

_____

_____

_____

_____

_____

_____

GLOSSARY

Collaborative research: The researcher and the participants, as a team, ask questions, design the project, interpret results, and write the research report.
Give your example:

_____

_____

_____

_____

Field notes: Observational notes where behaviors are recorded; see also methodological, personal, and theoretical notes.

Habituation: Participants and observers grow accustomed and get used to each others' presence so they are minimally affected by each other.

Give your example:

_____

_____

_____

_____

_____

Initial/preliminary observations: Those observations contacted at the very beginning of a project. They are used to debug and refine the observational plan.
Give your example:

_____

_____

_____

_____

Methodological notes: Notes made, as part of field notes, that help clarify issues related to method, such as logistics.

Nonparticipant observer: An observer who remains detached from the subjects that are being observed.
Contrast with *participant observer*:

_____

_____

_____

_____

Obtrusive: Describes a situation in which the observer or the procedure interferes with the normal course of events that are under observation.

Give your example:

Participant observer: An observer who wants to get an insider perspective by becoming a member of the group he or she is observing.

Contrast with *nonparticipant observer:*

Personal notes: Part of field notes, whereby the observer notes his or her own reactions to the observations being conducted.

Theoretical notes: Part of field notes that describe aspects of the observation that are relevant to the observer's theory.

5

Developing a Category System

CATEGORY CHOICE AS A THEORETICAL ACT

At this stage of the observational process we are ready to start thinking very specifically about the sorts of things we will actually be observing. In short, it is time to come up with a category or coding system. By a coding system, I mean the way in which we will organize those aspects of the stream of behavior that we choose to study. As I have noted at various points thus far, interaction between and among individuals is very complicated; there are lots of things going on at many different levels. To illustrate the levels of complexity, we will take the case of a mother and baby interacting around a storybook at bedtime. At a microlevel, we can be concerned with the gaze coordination of the mother and baby and develop a coding system that extracts aspects of the interaction that relate specifically to this issue. At another level, we may be interested in the heart rate of each participant at different points of the interaction. At a more macrolevel, we may be interested in the ways in which mothers end the stories and say goodnight to their children and develop a coding system that captures those aspects of the interaction.

Three points are immediately relevant here. First, interactions are immensely complex. Second, because of this complexity, a researcher must choose specific aspects of the interaction to study; one simply cannot describe everything. Third, and as a direct consequent of the first two points, all coding systems abstract aspects of interaction. That is, by taking behaviors from the context in which they occur and putting them into some coding or category system we lose some information. It should be the case that we are aware of what is lost and that loss is irrelevant to the questions we asked. If we are interested in the ways in which mothers end bedtime stories, coordination of gaze and heart rate throughout the story may be irrelevant and thus disposable information.

All of this is to say that our coding/categorization schemes should be driven by our questions and the ways in which these questions interface with the specific situation in which the observations will be made. Though this point may seem obvious it is often lost, so it seems worth some extended discussion. We may choose to develop a coding system to reflect specific questions we have in mind and our research context, or we may choose to use or adapt a coding system already developed by someone else.

A note of caution: If you choose someone else's system it may not fit. Very often researchers have developed systems that reflect their own theoretical orientations and the specifics of their own situations. As noted by Bakeman and Gottman (1986), a coding system is a theoretical statement; thus, to choose someone else's coding system assumes that you, too, share that orientation. Because of the implications of such a choice, it makes sense when choosing a coding system, even if it is borrowed from someone else, to do so only after you have determined the match between your specific research questions and those specified in extant coding systems.

USING OR ADAPTING SOMEONE ELSE'S CODING SYSTEM

A brief word about adopting, adapting, or borrowing extant category, or coding, systems is necessary. As noted previously, the use of a coding system should be theoretically consistent with other dimensions of the observational project. One must be aware of the degree to which the specific questions being asked by the researcher and the originator of the scheme are similar, enough that they can be answered with the same observational scheme. Use of the same coding system is obviously appropriate in cases of replication. It is also necessary that the coding system be useful in your specific situation. In short, the choice of an observational coding system should be integrated with all aspects of the study. If not, the results are of very limited utility.

There are numerous places where the researcher can find observational coding schemes and then determine their appropriateness. The most obvious place to look is in current research periodicals in which observational research is utilized. Some of these journal are *Animal Behavior, Child Development, Developmental Psychology,* and *Journal of Applied Developmental Psychology.* More dated but useful source books include the edited volume by Blurton Jones (1972), which includes numerous microlevel coding systems and Simon and Boyer's (1967) *Mirrors for Behavior.* More recent schemes for children's social behavior, language, and play are included in Pellegrini (1992).

A Sad Tale of Inappropriate Borrowing

By way of illustration I provide an example where a coding scheme was borrowed with little thought to these details. The example is from the area of children's play. A very popular coding scheme to capture the cognitive dimensions of preschool children's play was developed by Smilansky (1968). It included functional, constructive, dramatic, and game play. This system was developed based on preschool children's play in classrooms.

What would happen if a researcher, also interested in the study of children's play, were to use this system, with little preplanning, to study the play of elementary school children's outdoor play on playgrounds? Well, the first thing that would happen is that the researcher would find most forms of behavior on the playground do not fit into this system. For example, on playgrounds children engage in running, climbing, chasing, and play fighting. Where do these fit in the Smilansky system? They do not, yet they are probably play. Further, elementary school students often engage in games with rules and very infrequently engage in functional and constructive play; dramatic play occurs infrequently. Thus, 75% of the categories (i.e., functional, constructive, and dramatic) are less than appropriate for our target age group.

In short, borrowing a system with little preplanning is a mistake. As was shown in this example, if an observer were to borrow a coding system without first having asked the appropriate questions, he or she would have wasted time and energy. The observer would have spent considerable time actually collecting observational data only to find that the behavior being observed did not fit into the system; thus, the data would be close to useless. If one chose to use the data anyway, its low quality would be readily apparent and thus probably unacceptable at most levels, that is, unacceptable as a course project or as a published research report. A better strategy is to spend time initially on those steps that are necessary in choosing or developing a coding system. In the following section, I explicate a process that will minimize falling into this trap.

WHAT'S THE QUESTION?

The role of the question is central to the scientific enterprise of inquiring into the nature of things. The initial question puts the observer on a track of seeking its answer. Thus, questions determine what we see as relevant and what will be coded; consequently, the question and the resulting coding scheme are important (theoretical) acts. The process by which a question is developed or adapted is cybernetic in nature to the extent that questions are posed, refined, and then reposed. This process is represented in Fig. 5.1.

Initially, the question posed should be a *general* one and (obviously) one that is interesting to the investigator. For example, a primary school teacher may ask the question, what role does recess play have in the classroom attention of my students? The nature of the questions asked are often the result of a number of interrelated processes: reading the research literature relevant to the question, discussions with colleagues, children, and parents, and insights or hypotheses derived from experience.

1. General questions
   - based on reading and experience
2. Specific questions/hypotheses
   - based on reading and preliminary observations

FIG. 5.1   Question formulation process.

With these general questions in mind, researchers should then move toward *specific* questions. Movement from general to specific questions occurs in the context of more reading of the research literature relevant to the question and preliminary observation. That is, the specificity of the questions you asked about the general problem can and should be guided by what others have done in this specific area and one's own general observations. Reading about the ways in which other researchers have answered related questions enables a researcher to begin to understand the nature of the problem more clearly and the theoretical assumptions behind specific questions and coding schemes.

Take the example of recess and classroom attention introduced earlier. The related research literature suggests that many observational systems focus on children's level of physical activity when they are on the playground. For example, some researchers code the level of vigor of children's activity along a 3-point continuum. The theoretical assumption behind this type of system is that the level of physical activity exhibited on the playground should relate to classroom behavior (antecedent and subsequent). Theoretically, these assumptions are based on variants of Surplus Energy Theory whereby excess energy must be expended in order that after confinement, children can attend to sedentary seat work.

The initial question also becomes refocused based on general or preliminary observations with this question in mind. Although I say much more about these initial observations later in this chapter, for now suffice it to say that observing relevant situations with a general question in mind helps to refocus the question. For example, a person may observe that children are particularly restless (e.g., more physically active and less attentive) in class during a rainy week with no outdoor recess. Additionally, one may observe that on days when children have had unusually long recess periods, they become bored toward the end of the period and engage in an unusually large number of arguments. Thus, the researcher is now concerned not only with the presence or absence of recess but also with the duration of the confinement period before recess and the recess period itself.

The question is now refocused such that the observer is looking at the relation among the duration of the preceding sedentary task (like sitting at a desk in the classroom), attention, activity during that time, activity at recess, and attention and activity when children go back into the classroom after recess. The refined question then becomes, what is the relation between previous confinement and activity in classrooms and on the playground? Based on this refined question, the observer must pay closer attention to the activity dimensions of recess and classroom tasks. Before proceeding, however, he or she must decide on the level of specificity of the coding system necessary to answer the question.

COMING UP WITH CATEGORIES

After developing specific questions that we wish to answer, we must next consider the level of category specificity. There are at least three levels of description that we can consider in developing a coding scheme: physical descriptions, descriptions by

TABLE 5.1
Three Types of Categories

Category	Description	Example
Physical	Muscle contraction	Wide smile
Consequence	Stimulus orientation	Makes friends
Relational	Environment relations	Group size

consequence, and relational descriptions (Martin & Bateson, 1993). These levels of categorization, and illustrative examples, are displayed in Table 5.1.

In each case we aspire to group together those behaviors that belong together in some reasonable way. What is reasonable, however, may be specific to a certain theory; therefore, (again) theoretical assumptions continue to exercise influence. *Physical descriptions* are descriptions of muscular contractions and are usually expressed in terms of degree, strength, and patterning (Hinde, 1980). For example, we could describe certain vigorous motor behaviors in terms of patterns of rough play. Physical descriptions are usually grouped together, or classified, in terms of their co-occurrence in space and time. The procedure by which they are grouped should be based on some theory and objective processes, such as factor analysis or Q-sorts. For example, we would group together under the heading of rough-and-tumble play all those physical behaviors (e.g., smiling, open-hand beat, run, jump, kick at) that co-occur during vigorous outdoor play.

Descriptions by consequence on the other hand, involve the orientation of a specific set of behaviors toward a certain outcome or consequence (Hinde, 1980). Rather than the co-occurrence of individual behaviors, a specific outcome is chosen and we look at the behaviors leading to it; thus, behaviors that lead to the same consequence belong in the same category. For example, we might look at the specific behaviors that lead to children interacting in a specific type of activity, like affiliating with peers. It may be the case that we group together gentle push, running, and smiling under the label of affiliative chase.

When choosing between these two specific levels of categorization, observers must be aware of the costs and benefits associated with each. The use of physical descriptions was originally proposed in child study by a group of ethologists (e.g., Blurton Jones, 1972) who considered many behavioral categories used in the child development literature as too subjective. This group of ethologists generally believed that the categories used by psychologists and educators were rooted in introspection, not in observations of children's behaviors. Their remedy was physical descriptions. These descriptions, however, are often too cumbersome for observers to conduct; there are often too many details to attend to.

Such microlevel analyses may miss patterns that are more conspicuous at a macrolevel of analysis. We know, for example, that interactions are rife with miscues to the extent that we try something, then change in mid-stream. Conversational analyses provide particularly good examples of miscues; for example, we may observe lots of self-corrections (at the microlevel) but they are all in service of mutual understanding (at the macrolevel). Thus, only by attending to more macrolevels are we able to make sense of the pattern of the interaction. If we were to attend to the microlevel, we may miss this point.

Consequential relations group behaviors into meaningful (rather macrolevel) categories that imply some motives or intent for the behavior. That children run and hit with others implies that they are engaging in chase. This level of explanation is very nice to aspire to. The down side of consequential grouping is equally obvious: Consequential considerations have biases. We may be considering a specific consequence as the goal of a set of behaviors, such as playful affiliation being the consequence of wrestling, when in fact there is another goal to which the behavior is directed, such as dominance exhibition. The same affiliative behaviors would be observed but with a very different interpretation. By way of possible remedy, preliminary observations should utilize relatively objective terms (like physical descriptions) to describe behavior and consequences. The use of relatively objective language enables reconsideration of original intent. Later in this chapter, use of such terms is discussed.

The last level of categorization involves describing individuals in *relation* to their environment (Martin & Bateson, 1993). In this case, individuals are described in terms of where they are or with whom they are interacting. Instead of describing motor activities or consequences of behavior, researchers employing this level of categorization consider where the individuals are and with whom they are doing it. By way of illustration, let us start with describing the physical environmental relations. As earlier examples were drawn from children on the playground, I continue in that arena. Relational descriptions of children on the playground might involve describing where on the playground children spend time. At a gross level, we might classify all behavior on the playground as play, simply because it is play time.

At another level we might be concerned with behaviors that occur in different aspects of the playground. For example, do children spend a specific amount of time on swings, climbing structures, or on walkways? We might also be concerned with the sorts of behaviors exhibited in these locations. Our theoretical orientation might lead us to look more specifically at different segments of the recess period and how environmental relations vary across these segments. For example, do children tend to congregate near the building, on walkways, toward the end of the recess period? Is play more vigorous at the start of recess than toward the end?

Relations can also be described in terms of social configurations. For example, what is the size of the group of kindergarten children who tend to play together at recess? What is the gender composition of groups of children at recess?

It would be interesting, depending on the nature of one's question of course, to combine various types of categorization systems. For example, we might combine relational and consequential systems to examine the extent to which groups are integrated by gender when they engage in certain types of activities, like chase or games with rules.

At this point we should have a general idea, based on our reading and some informal observations, of the questions we will ask and the type of categories that we will use. Now we must enter the field to look at the behaviors related to our problem. This will allow us to generate a specific coding scheme.

CATEGORIES FROM PRELIMINARY OBSERVATIONS

With knowledge of the question in mind, as well as consideration of the level of specificity to which an observer aspires, the researcher enters the relevant field to generate a specific coding scheme. Again, decisions about questions and possible dimensions of coding systems are tied to the related observational and theoretical literature. As I noted in preceding chapters, however, before this stage it is important to determine whether the phenomena of interest are observable at a particular site. With this question answered affirmatively, one is ready to observe.

Hanging Out

The first stages of the observational process involve hanging out, or spending lots of time in a setting looking at a variety of things. An observer takes into the field the research questions and the level of categorization to which he or she aspires. With these "sensitizing concepts" (Patton, 1990, p. 218) in mind, the observer looks at those things that he or she thinks will be interesting. Again, I stress the fact that one cannot observe everything; there is simply too much out there. Furthermore, observers, as human beings do not go into the field tabula rasa; they have guiding concepts, questions, and category levels to provide some structure to their observations.

It probably makes most sense, in the very first observations, for the observer to not use any types of recording devices, such as paper and pen, tape recorder, or video camera. This rule is especially important to follow if observers will actually be in the field of observation, as compared to a remote site, such as a one-way viewing booth or filming from a distance. The reason is straightforward enough: The participants must get used to an observer before introduction of another strange entity.

During this hanging out time an observer should be thinking about the question and categories and the ways in which they are realized in these preliminary observations. Are the categories capturing the essence of what kids are doing? Are the categories too involved? Not involved enough? Further, he or she should be noting the participants who exhibit those behaviors of interest and the location of these acts. Also note the location of these acts. Immediately after leaving the field the observer should either write out or dictate into a tape recorder any thoughts on these processes.

Writing (Saying) It Out

After participants have habituated, the observer can start recording behavior in the field. To this end, most students of behavioral observation suggest writing out, in expository form, what is seen. In some cases, it may be easier for the observer to whisper these descriptions into a tape recorder than to write them out. In my own observations of children on playgrounds, I have used tape recorders, not notes, because the tape recorder enabled me to record more information than if I were writing. Further, I didn't have to take time to look at the paper to record my thoughts; I could keep my eyes on the subject matter at hand. Again, we cannot write or record everything; we let our questions and category levels serve as a guide.

The form that these notes or dictations take should be such that *objective descriptions* of participants behavior are recorded along with interpretations and notes on the phenomena (Corsaro, 1981; Patton, 1990). Objective descriptions of behavior (or low inference if objectivity is questioned) are those in which the level of inference made by the observer is kept to a minimum. Indeed, this level is close to noting physical descriptions of behaviors. In Table 5.2, I outline a number of contrasts between objective and subjective language used to describe the same behaviors.

The objective descriptions in the left-hand column are physical descriptions of behavior with minimal inference. By that I mean the observer is not inferring intent or motivation for specific acts; he or she is describing in terms of movements as seen. Objectivity in the descriptors chosen is crucial at this stage to the extent that, a newcomer to a specific field probably does not understand fully what it is he or she is observing. Objective descriptions help to reformulate the questions to reflect more accurately the nature of the phenomena being observed. For example, if the observer initially considered a description by consequence category system, he or she may have grouped behaviors inappropriately with inferential descriptors. Objective descriptors allow a person to evaluate the degree to which the initial categories are true.

Let us take, for example, the use of the terms *constructive play* and *putting blocks in a row* as contrastive cases. Obviously, in using constructive play to describe what a child is doing one is making inferences about what the child is doing; the observer is inferring a consequence of an action or set of actions. This inference may be based on the fact that the child is alone and not vocalizing about his actions, so he must be constructing, not doing something else. Thus, this set of behaviors may be incorrectly classified. In a later observation, the same child exhibiting the same physical behaviors with a peer may seem to be engaging in pretend play.

Putting blocks in a row, on the other hand, describes the same action with minimal inference. Such a description, when tied to other description such as the child moving a block around the floor saying "brmmmmmm," allows a researcher to reconstitute the constructive and dramatic play categories. One can maximize the likelihood of descriptions being objective if the actual behaviors involved are described. Direct quotes from participants are also very helpful in generating initial descriptions.

TABLE 5.2
Objective and Subjective Descriptors

Objective	Subjective
Wide smile	Having fun
Open hand hit-at	Fighting
Paints on paper and table	Sloppy painting
Putting blocks in a row	Constructive play

It is useful when entering the field to use the observational procedures recommended by Corsaro (1981) and defined in the previous chapter. For example, methodological notes can be used by the observer to supplement the objective descriptions (Corsaro, 1981). As suggested in the preceding chapter, these notes are good complements to the descriptive notes in that they provide some guidance to the ways in which observations should be conducted in the future. In the example of blocks, a methodological note might suggest that playing alone with blocks is not necessarily constructive because children do not talk often when they are alone. When children are alone, we should look for other indicators to determine the type of play they are engaged in.

Personal notes also complement initial descriptions (Corsaro, 1981). An observer may note, for example, that he or she has very difficult time observing in the block area because it is too dark; thus, the observer cannot distinguish different types of behavior very well. Theoretical notes, too, are helpful. In this case, one could note that the frequently reported finding that children playing alone with blocks engage in constructive play may be misleading. It may be due to the fact that when alone, children do not talk. Thus, the behavior is not coded as dramatic because no utterances indicate fantasy.

After these descriptions and various notes are taken, the observer should then try to square this new information with the questions asked and the level of categorization considered. The research is now ready to outline some specific categories.

THE SPECIFIC CATEGORY SYSTEM

The first rule of thumb in generating a specific category system is to keep the system tied to the specific question. The second rule of thumb is to keep the system only as complicated as is necessary to answer the question. In this section, I pose two separate questions and walk through the process by which a coding system is developed. Before that is done, however, I address some technical properties of categories.

Categories should be homogeneous, mutually exclusive, and sometimes exhaustive (Bakeman & Gottman, 1986; Martin & Bateson, 1993). By *homogeneous* I mean that all subcomponents of a category should be related to the same construct. That is, they should be providing different exemplars of the same phenomenon; there should not be any "lumps," or outliers. By way of simile, we can compare the homogeneity of a bottle of homogenized milk with nonhomogenized milk. In the former case the cream is evenly distributed throughout the bottle. In the latter case, the cream and the milk are separate, though both are in the same bottle. The components of individual categories should be like the homogenized milk, with individual components all being part of the same whole. For example, a homogeneous category for rough-and-tumble play might include smile, hit, and run. All these behaviors co-occur and note different dimensions of the same category.

A nonhomogeneous (heterogeneous?) category includes the components already noted as well as outliers, like bite and punch. Again, category homogeneity is determined empirically (i.e., to what degree to they actually co-occur) and theoretically (i.e., can they be related for some plausible reasons). If categories are not homogeneous, they are confusing; aggregating across dissimilar components of categories may hide systematic patterns in the data.

Categories should also be *mutually exclusive*. By this I mean that the individual categories should be measuring only one thing at a time, not more than one thing; behaviors should fit into one and only one category. Thus, a behavior cannot simultaneously be coded as both rough-and-tumble play (R&T) and aggression; it goes into only one category. Similarly, take the case of having two categories, social interaction and conversation. They are certainly conceptually and probably empirically interrelated to the extent that conversation is a subset of social interaction. In this case, new codes are needed. Either conversation should be collapsed into social interaction or two social interaction categories, verbal and nonverbal, should be created. That categories are mutually exclusive is particularly important for data analyses. If different categories are measuring the same or related categories, we are limited in our ability to say anything about the separate categories.

It is often the case, however, that one set of behaviors can be coded in a number of different ways. For example, rough-and-tumble play can be also be categorized as vigorous play or cooperative play. With preschool boys much of it can probably be coded as dramatic play. That we choose to categorize it as R&T, rather than the alternatives, is a theoretical matter. In terms of mutual exclusivity of categories, by extension, we should not have vigorous play or cooperative play categories defined such that R&T could fit into either.

Lastly, category systems can be *exhaustive*. By exhaustive I mean that we have categories that can account for all the behavior that occurs in a particular setting. I say categories can be rather than must be, because it is really optional. It is nice to have an exhaustive system if we want to construct an ethogram of a particular context to the extent that we have a full index of behavior in that area. Exhaustive systems are necessary primarily to look at sequences of behavior. Specifically, to look at the probability of an individual behavior following another, one must have categories for all possible behaviors that could be observed. A shortcut here involves having a dust bin category, such as other behavior, which accounts for less than relevant behavior. Alternatively, observers could also note unusual behaviors that occur but are not coded. In short, behavior should be coded into categories that are homogeneous and independent of each other.

TWO EXAMPLES OF CATEGORY SYSTEM DEVELOPMENT

In this section, I discuss the process of developing two separate coding systems. In the first case I address the way in which an observer can use a variant of an existing coding system to answer a question. I chose this specific scenario because it seems to be fairly common for observers at all levels to adopt an existing model. In the second example, I discuss the development of a system from the bottom up.

Starting With an Extant System

Let's say that you are motivated to conduct an observation because you are interested in the ways in which different preschool-age children play together with different toys. You, as kindergarten teacher, may be concerned with using play and play centers as a way to stimulate children's development. That query serves as the initial, general question. With this general question in mind, you then start to read the play and toy literatures. As part of your reading, you find out that play is defined in various ways; thus, your initial reading is aimed at a more exact definition of what is meant by play. This clarification of a definition of play is crucial as it will, in turn, provide a basis for a way in which you code play behavior. That is, the components of a definition of play may also serve as dimensions for codes that define play.

As you read the definition of play literature, you find out that the play of preschool children has been extensively described according to both social and cognitive dimensions in a relatively simple scheme generated by Ken Rubin (see Rubin, Fein, & Vandenberg, 1983). The components of the scheme involve a description of play along cognitive dimensions (e.g., functional, constructive, dramatic) and social dimensions (e.g., solitary, parallel, and interactive). This scheme, as you find out, has also been used to describe the sophistication (in cognitive and social terms) of the different forms of play. For example, you find out that children engaging in interactive-dramatic and solitary-constructive play tend to score higher on social and cognitive measures than children engaging in solitary-dramatic play. You also find out, by reading and by observing children in your classroom, that specific contextual configurations such as specific toys influence the levels of play on this scheme.

At this point you reformulate your question to reflect your new knowledge. It becomes, How does the social-cognitive level of play vary in different play settings? Thus, you seem to be working with a very general and inferential definition of play (that is, a description by consequence). You take the observation scheme and begin to use it to conduct preliminary observations. Thus, you have these nine categories (i.e., three cognitive categories X three social categories) in your head as you observe children and write down descriptions. Indeed, you may have even constructed a matrix, as displayed in Fig. 5.2, by which to classify the behaviors.

As you observe, however, you recognize some things that do not seem to fit very well into those nine categories. For example, where do you put children's playful wrestling? You decide to add a category called rough play; now you have 10

	Solitary	Parallel	Interactive
Functional			
Constructive			
Dramatic			

FIG. 5.2 An example of a play coding matrix.

categories. You also observe tremendous within-category variability for one category: interactive-dramatic. For example, within the interactive-dramatic category, you notice that some children's make believe play is very well integrated. Other children's play, although interactive-dramatic, is more fragmented, consisting of a series of minimally related play themes. Thus, the problem becomes that the system seems to be too macro for you: It does not differentiate children's level of pretend coordination within the interactive-dramatic category.

Now you need to come up with a complementary coding system. That is, you may use the nine code system plus the rough play category and develop a complementary system. That complementary system, in turn, is based on your reformulated questions: What are the social-cognitive dimensions of children's play with different toys? How integrated is the interactive-dramatic play of children? You then review the literature specific to integrating play themes while observing. You may then decide that integration is best measured by interconnected language. Thus, your complementary coding system includes linguistic measures: response–nonresponse sequences, topic match between initiation and response, and disagreements. If the original nine plus one categories and the complement to the interactive-dramatic category are sufficient to answer your question, you now have a coding system. You should recognize that your system is homogeneous, exhaustive, but not mutually exclusive. The interaction categories are a subset of interactive-dramatic behavior; thus, these categories are interdependent and should be used as dimensions of one construct: interactive-dramatic play.

Developing an Original Category System

Suppose you begin with the general question of whether children's rough-and-tumble play escalates into aggression. To answer this question you begin by reading the literature on R&T and aggression because you need to have categories for observing each. You discover by reading and observing that aggression and R&T have been conceptualized as very different constructs: R&T is playful and fun for children, and aggression is harmful. You also observe that when children are doing the former they often smile or laugh (a dimension of a coding system) and in the latter they often frown or grimace. Furthermore, R&T play generally has children alternating roles, say between the top and bottom positions in wrestling, whereas aggression is not reciprocal but is unilateral. Both R&T and aggression, however, involve vigorous physical contact (such as hitting) and large motor activity (such as running). At this point, based on initial readings and observations, you have the skeleton of a coding system that involves affect (e.g., smile or frown), roles (e.g., reciprocal or unilateral), and physical contact behavior. The components of these categories are micro, to the degree that some describe physical behaviors and smiles, and consequential, to the degree that roles are being described.

With this level of categorization in mind, you continue your preliminary observations, looking specifically for behaviors that meet your criteria. As you observe you find different types of R&T. For example, you find that certain vigorous behaviors tend to co-occur: smile, push, hit, run away from, run after. In other cases, other physically vigorous behaviors co-occur: smile, hit, kick, grapple, roll on ground, top position, bottom position. You have arrived at a new distinction (and consequently, two new categories) in rough play: chase and play fighting. Could it be, you refocus, that play fighting, not chase, is likely to escalate into aggression? At this point, you have three categories (i.e., chase, play fighting, and aggression) that are homogeneous and mutually exclusive. The level of description is, for the most part, at the physical description level. You have your categories and are almost ready to observe.

I say almost because your question was a sequential question to the extent that you asked about the escalation of R&T into aggression, that is, the probability of different forms of R&T leading to aggression (see Chapter 10 for a discussion of sequential analyses). As I noted earlier, in order to answer sequential questions, your observational system must be exhaustive. At this point you must decide the degree to which you are interested in describing all the other behaviors that you have observed. If you are interested in this, your question has changed to include not only the relation between R&T and aggression but also all the other behaviors that occur on the playground. If you are not interested in the larger question you should merely create an "other" category. Your system would thus include play fighting, chasing, aggression, and other behaviors.

SUMMARY AND CONCLUSIONS

In this chapter I have outlined a process through which an observer comes up with a set of categories by which behaviors will be categorized during observations. The most basic concern in developing a category system is in the nature of the question being asked: The categories that are used should be aimed specifically toward answering that question. Asking a question is a very personal and important process in that it is what a researcher considers to be interesting. This question, in turn, determines the way in which he or she will conduct subsequent work in this specific area. To borrow someone else's coding requires a great deal of thought. One can borrow only to the degree to which the observer and the originator agree on very important issues of theory and method. Thus, it makes most sense to spend lots of time explicating a good question. Is the question similar to those who have already developed observational systems? Are the children of the same age and social circumstances? If so, use of an existing scheme may make sense. There are no shortcuts.

An observer may, on the other hand, choose to develop a new category system. These categories should reflect a specific question or theory as well as the idiosyncracies of the situation. Categories systems should be sensitive to all these demands in order to capture what the participants are doing. In this regard observers who use inductive category systems are trying to develop systems that are maximally sensitive to the observational context. Thus, at this level, there is minimal difference between insiders and outsiders approaches to observational methods.

THINGS TO THINK ABOUT

1. Take the case of reading books to children before bedtime. Generate a list of three general questions that could be used as a basis for an observational study.

_____

_____

_____

_____

_____

_____

1a. For each general question, generate one specific question.

_____

_____

_____

_____

_____

1b. For each specific question, list five general behavioral categories that could be used to help answer the question.

_____

_____

_____

_____

_____

_____

_____

1c. For each general category, list three specific observable behaviors.

_____

_____

_____

_____

_____

_____

2. Go to a neighborhood playground. Observe one group of children while they are playing some game. Try observing their behaviors in terms of structure, consequence, and relations.

_____

_____

_____

_____

_____

_____

2a. Procedurally, collect descriptive data in various media. First, look for the whole game period and then try to recreate the behaviors from memory. Then take notes as behaviors occur. Finally, try talking into a tape recorder.

_____

_____

_____

_____

_____

_____

2b. Observe another group of children play the same game. Do the descriptions of these behaviors resemble those generated earlier?

_____

_____

_____

_____

_____

_____

2c. How would you go about finding out when children do certain things at home without your actually being in the home?

_____

_____

_____

_____

_____

_____

_____

3. Take each of the nine categories of the social cognitive play matrix discussed in this chapter. For each, list five possible physical descriptions and five possible relational descriptions.

_____

_____

_____

_____

_____

_____

_____

GLOSSARY

Category/Coding System: The way in which behaviors are organized into meaningful units.

Category, Exhaustive: A grouping that accounts for all the behaviors under observation.

Category, Homogeneous: A grouping wherein all subcomponents of the category are conceptually and empirically interrelated.
Give your example:

_____

_____

_____

_____

_____

_____

Category, Mutually Exclusive: A grouping wherein the individual categories do not overlap such that a behavior is assigned to one and only one category.
Give your example:

_____

_____

_____

_____

_____

_____

Cybernetic: A inquiry system whereby a question is influenced by subsequent inquiry; this inquiry, in turn, becomes redefined with experience.
Give your example:

_____

_____

_____

_____

_____

_____

Description, Consequence: A category based on descriptions of the endpoint of numerous behaviors. For example, affiliation could be a consequential category of a number of behaviors such as chase, follow, invite, or smile.

Give your example:

_____

_____

_____

_____

_____

Description, Physical: A category based on descriptions of physical movements and muscle tension or contraction. For example, a physical description for the category exploration would include increased heart rate, neutral facial expression (i.e., straight mouth), and deliberate gaze.

Give your example:

_____

_____

_____

_____

_____

Description, Relational: A category based on where the subject is located, either in terms of physical location or group composition. For example, cooperative interaction occurs in the block area of a classroom.

Give your example:

_____

_____

_____

_____

_____

_____

Ethogram: A thorough description of behaviors exhibited by individuals in specific situations.

Factor analyses: A group of statistical techniques that determine the extent to which individual behaviors or other variables can be grouped together into larger categories. For example, we could determine through factor analyses the degree to which certain physical descriptions belong in distinctive categories.

Hypothesis: An educated guess by a researcher about what will happen.
Give your example:

_____

_____

_____

_____

_____

_____

Macrolevel Category: A category system that has a number of subcomponents; for example, aggression is a macrolevel category with microlevel components such as hit, kick, and bite.
Give your example:

_____

_____

_____

_____

_____

_____

Microlevel Category: A category system that has few subcomponents and is often based on physical descriptions and low inference; for example, a microlevel category for attention might include heart rate and gaze.

Give your example:

_____

_____

_____

_____

_____

_____

_____

Objective Descriptions: Descriptions that are low inference and consequently are often based on physical descriptions and not on inferences about motivation or intent.

Give your example:

_____

_____

_____

_____

_____

_____

Q-sort: A research technique used by observers or participants who put descriptors into categories they think are relevant.

Give your example:

_____

_____

_____

_____

_____

_____

Sensitizing Concepts: Questions and categories that observers take with them into the field as they conduct their preliminary observations. These concepts direct them to relevant behaviors and events.

Give your example:

_____

_____

_____

_____

_____

_____

6

Measuring, Sampling, and Recording Behavior

In this chapter, I address some very specific procedures involved in measuring behavior. As I noted in Chapter 2, researchers make basic choices about the ways in which they choose to measure behavior. The outsider approach, in contrast to the insider approach, measures behavior by degree. In this chapter, I continue the orientation by describing some of the ways in which categories can be measured. By measured I mean the different ways in which categories can be quantified. Next, I describe the ways in which the categories can be sampled from the stream of ongoing behavior and then recorded. Specific measurement concerns covered include frequency, duration, latency, pattern, and intensity.

MEASURING BEHAVIOR

I discuss five ways in which behavior can be measured: duration, frequency, pattern, latency, and intensity (Martin & Bateson, 1993; Suen & Ary, 1989). These measures, with corresponding definitions and examples, are displayed in Table 6.1. Although there are variations on the measures of behavior presented in the table, these five measures are a sound basis by which to measure behavior and develop more refined measures.

To begin, we should note the time period or *session length*, during which the observations are occurring because it is an important qualifier of the measures we generate. Much more is said about the length of individual observational sessions later in this chapter, when I discuss sampling issues. Suffice it to say that as observers we may be concerned with sampling either specific behaviors, such as aggression, whenever they occur during a specified period or we may be interested in sampling behaviors across a specified time period, say aggression during a 20-minute time period. In both the behavior and the time sampling cases, the issue of session length is relevant. Let us say for the purpose of the following examples presented that we are observing children during 20-minute free play periods in their classrooms.

TABLE 6.1
Measures of Behavior

Measure	Definition	Example
Duration	Time of a behavior pattern	R&T bouts are 20 seconds
Frequency	Number of behaviors/time unit	3 hits/hour
Pattern	Behavior across time	Hit/push/hit/bite
Latency	Time from x to behavior	10 seconds from seeing word to reading it
Intensity	Degree of amplitude	Vigor rated 1, 2, 3

With this as background, we start with the first measure: *duration*. Duration is a measure of the length of a behavior during a specific session, and it is usually measured in terms of seconds (and parts thereof), minutes, and hours. Duration can refer to the interval from the onset (or beginning) of a behavior to the offset (or termination) of that behavior. Taking the 20-minute session length, we might say that for a specific child the duration from onset to offset of drawing was 4 minutes. This could be expressed as 4 minutes per 20 minutes and defined as *total duration*.

Mean durations are averages of total durations, across individuals or within individuals, across sessions. Let us say that we observed four children whose total durations of drawing were 3, 2, 5, and 10 minutes. The mean duration would be the sum of these four durations (20 minutes) divided by 4, or 5 minutes. *Relative*, or *proportional duration*, is the duration divided by the session length: 4/20 or .20. Whereas the relative measure is a timeless index of specific behavior, the total and mean durations are explicitly stated in terms of time (Martin & Bateson, 1993).

A complement to duration measures is the measurement of *frequency*. Frequency is a measure of the occurrence of specific behaviors within an observational session. For example, perhaps during our hypothetical 20-minute session, we observed 6 R&T bouts. Discussion of frequency in relation to the length of the observational session becomes very clear again. Without consideration of the session length, the number 6 becomes almost meaningless. Does the 6 mean that it was observed 6 times in 1 minute, 5 minutes, 30 minutes, or 3 hours? Obviously, the 6 has very different meaning in each of these cases. Frequency, then, should be discussed in terms relative to the session length; thus, frequency could really be expressed as a rate to the extent that we measure frequency per time unit. In these examples, we have different rates of R&T per minute.

Frequency and duration are very common measures of behavior. Indeed, it is often interesting to collect both types of measure of behavioral categories. Obviously, the nature of one's questions should drive the type of measures used, but frequency and duration can sometimes provide complementary information for specific behaviors. Both, for example, are excellent measures of what individuals spend their time doing and, correspondingly, the degree to which individuals expend resources. Frequency tells us something about the rate of expenditure, whereas duration tells us the extent to which the expenditure is sustained. It may be the case, for example, that children frequently run in the course of recess, but the duration of each bout is brief. Longer durations may be exhibited in other types of behaviors, such as games.

Patterns of behavior are measures of specific categories of behavior across time. These patterns need not, however, be expressed in terms of a specific time interval; their order of occurrence may be noted with no mention of time between acts. For example, during our 20-minute observation session we may observe that children's play is patterned in the following way: chase, push, chased, hit, chase. Although we note that this took place during a 20-minute session, we may choose not to note the actual duration of the components of the pattern. If we choose to add a temporal dimension we can add the duration of each of the individual play components to the total play bout. The time dimension may be useful, and with the use of mechanical recording devices (discussed in Chapter 10) it is increasingly easy to record time. By tying patterns to a temporal dimension we come closer to representing its actual occurrence.

Latency, like duration, is a measure of time. With latency, we measure the time from the focal individual's exposure to a relevant stimulus to the behavioral response. Some very common examples of latency measures from the education and cognitive psychology literatures respectively, include wait time and reaction time. Wait time is the latency between when an instructor asks a question of a student and when the teacher talks again, assuming that the student does not talk in the interval. The latency in this case is a matter of a few seconds. Reaction time is a measure of the latency between the presentation of a stimulus, such a word to be read, and the child's reading of the word. Reaction time is usually expressed in terms of microseconds. We assume that longer latencies indicate that mental processing is occurring. In the cases of 10- and 15-microsecond latencies to two presented words, we could assume that the second was more difficult for the children to the extent that he or she took more time to process it.

Intensity is the last measure, and it is probably the most difficult to measure. Intensity is a measure of degree or amplitude, rather than frequency (Martin & Bateson, 1993). Following the R&T example, intensity could be measured as high, medium, or low. Because such judgments can be very subjective and consequently unreliable, it is very important to specify the ways in which we differentiate levels of intensity. Martin and Bateson (1993) suggested using local rates as one measure of intensity. By local rates they meant the number of components of a behavior that occur within a certain time interval. Take the case of R&T again, defined as having 10 components (e.g., tease, hit/kick, chase, poke, sneak up, carry child, pile on, play fight, hold/push). A local rate could be the number of components that occur within a certain period, say 2 minutes. More intense ratings would be those that had more components than less intense ratings. Of course, this type of measure (implicitly) assumes that individual components are equal in terms of intensity. That is, by adding together different units, they are all treated as if they make equal contributions to the whole. This may be problematic, however, if individual components are not equal; for example, if we had run and walk as components of chase we could not treat them as equal, as run is more intense (e.g., evidenced by a higher heart rate) than walking.

One way to address this issue is to measure intensity by consequence (Martin & Bateson, 1993). In such cases we could measure the result of a specific behavior. Take the running example. We could measure the distance covered during an interval, the number of calories burned, or heart rate as consequential measures. Whereas some of these measures may be problematic and obtrusive to use (e.g., heart rate), others, such as distance, are not. Distance can be measured, for example, by dividing the observation area into graph-like plots so we can note the number of plots covered during a specified time. A bit more difficult and obtrusive is the use of actometers. *Actometers* are mechanical devices attached to a foot or hand that record level of activity. Such measures may, however, be both impractical and undesirable to use, thus compounding the problem of objectively measuring intensity.

One way in which I have dealt with this conundrum in my own research is to use definitions of intensity that have been objectively related to these more obtrusive measures in previous research (i.e., the validity of the measures was established by relating it concurrently to another measure). Specifically, in my research on children's recess behavior, I am interested in the level of vigor of their behavior, a measure of intensity. Although vigor can be most objectively measured with an actometer or heart rate, it can also be measured by drawing on research that measured vigor with observational criteria and then related those criteria to actometer readings. In my case, I coded vigor along 9 dimensions. Categories 1 to 3 were coded when the participant was lying down, with high, medium, and low ratings assigned to specific sets of behaviors. Categories 4 to 6 and 7 to 9, respectively, referred to sets of behavior while participants were sitting and standing. Each measure also had a corresponding caloric expenditure value. Thus, intensity could be an interesting but difficult component of behavior to measure objectively.

In this portion of the chapter I have addressed specific ways in which behavior can be measured. As I noted, these measures are generally concerned with behavior along temporal and frequency dimensions. At one level, these measures can be described in terms of states or events (Bakeman & Gottman, 1986; Martin & Bateson, 1993). States and events are differentiated in terms of duration. States are usually longer in duration than are events. For example, R&T bouts may be considered states, whereas a cry may be considered an event. Events are measured along frequency and intensity dimensions, whereas states are usually measured by time and pattern dimensions.

I stressed that the relative nature of specific measures should be considered. For example, in reporting frequencies, those frequencies relative to a specific time interval are important to note. Similarly, relative scores may be necessary in cases where individuals have not all been be observed for equal periods. In this case, relative scores, too, are important. Behaviors relative to total observational time for each individual can still be used. In other cases, individual components of behavior, such as push, can be reported relative to the sum of all other behaviors. These procedures simply aim to equalize children's scores in cases of unequal frequency of observations.

In the next section, I discuss those sampling and recording strategies used to extract behaviors from their stream so that they can be measured.

SAMPLING AND RECORDING BEHAVIOR

Sampling Behavior

The notion of sampling is crucial to understanding one specific way in which behavior can be studied. Sampling refers to the degree to which we choose to observe all that can be observed. All that can be observed is referred to as the universe of behavior. We sample behavior because it is neither practical nor necessary to observe all behavior.

By way of example, take the familiar example of watching television on election night. We view the television with predictions being made about who will win in a certain area before the election is over. How can this be done? Through sampling. That is, surveys are conducted on a sample of all voters. Inferences about all voters (i.e., the universe, or population, of voters) are made based on what a sample of the voters does. We can make an inference (or prediction) of what the whole group will do based on our knowledge of a sample of that population.

Obviously, the more we sample, the more we approximate the universe; therefore, larger samples are generally more accurate than smaller samples. By accurate I mean more accurately reflect the nature of the whole universe. Size of the sample, however, is not enough to guarantee an accurate sample. Systematic rules of sampling must be followed. Correspondingly, specific sampling rules are necessary to derive the measures outlined at the beginning of this chapter. Following Martin and Bateson (1993; see also Altmann, 1974, for another and often cited discussion of these issues), I separate sampling rules, or those rules that extract behavior from its ongoing stream, from recording rules, or how the behaviors are recorded.

Sampling, like the measures discussed earlier, can be generally grouped according to behavior or time sampling. Behavior, or event, sampling involves observing all occurrences of a specific behavior. Thus, we become concerned with a specific behavior occurring or not occurring within a certain observational period. Behavior or event sampling is most useful when we are interested in a relatively infrequently occurring behavior; thus, we look for it and only it and record it when it occurs. Aggression is commonly studied with event sampling because it does not occur that frequently (at least in some contexts). Furthermore, event sampling is useful when we are interested in the structure of the event itself; we want to record it from beginning to end.

The time-oriented methods are concerned with dividing up the observational period into time units and making observations (or sampling) within those units. The motivation for time orientation is simple: It is often impractical, and indeed unnecessary, to conduct observations for long and uninterrupted periods of time. Thus, time-oriented sampling involves extracting bits of behavior from their temporal stream. As a result of our taking behaviors out of ongoing behavioral streams, it becomes very important to make clear and systematic decisions about the ways in which it will be done. After all, it is this sample of behavior that will be used to make inferences about the universe of behavior. If we choose an unrepresentative sample of behavior it will yield information that does not represent the universe of behavior.

For example, if we choose to sample the life of a university professor only from 11:30 a.m. until 12:30 p.m., Monday through Friday, we will get only one type of information that probably is not very representative of what this person does during the rest of the day. In this case more sampling points, say at 9:30, 10:30, 11:30, 2:30, and 4:30 would give a better, more representative picture. The point is that to achieve representativeness we should have numerous samples of behavior within days and numerous observations across different days. In this way we maximize the likelihood that we are gathering a representative sample of individuals' behavior.

I discuss three sampling rules: ad libitum, focal person, and scan sampling (Martin & Bateson, 1993). *Ad libitum* sampling is not systematic to the extent that it has the observer not following a prespecified set of rules. The observer watches what and whom he or she sees fit to observe. This method is useful in the initial stages of observational work (see Chapter 4), to the extent that it helps the observer get a very general picture of what exists in the observational field. That is, it gives the observer some flavor of the context. The problem with ad libitum sampling is that observers tend to see the most obvious and most visible sets of individuals and behaviors. Consequently, this procedure is extremely susceptible to the influence of observer bias.

Focal person sampling involves choosing one individual and observing him or her for a specified period. For example, in my R&T research I use focal person (child) sampling for 3-minute intervals such that during a 20-minute recess period I observe in predetermined random order at least six separate children. During each 3-minute interval, I record all relevant behaviors of the focal child, as well as other children and adults with whom the focal child is interacting. This form of recording is known as continuous recording and is discussed later in this chapter.

Choice of an appropriate observational interval depends on what one is interested in. If an observer is interested in particular patterns of interaction, the choice should be at least as long as, and possibly longer than, those types of interaction of interest. If a person is interested in pretend play themes, he or she should gauge the length of the theme and make the interval at least that long. Often times, however, a focal child, "disappears"; this is particularly true if observations take place outdoors. In these cases, the observer must have a rule, such as stop observation if child is out of sight for 30 seconds. Consequently, measures would be a proportion of time observed.

Focal sampling, especially when tied to continuous recording, is very useful to construct thorough descriptions of a sample. With this method, we can derive numerous measures and accurately reconstruct the behavior of focal participants.

The downside of focal sampling is that it is time consuming (Sackett, 1978). That is, if we are observing a large number of individuals, use of focal sampling involves a number of discrete observations. This problem may, however, be minimized with numerous observers and video-recording equipment (Sackett, 1978). With numerous observers, separate observers can be assigned to separate focal children. With videotapes, more than one child can be recorded simultaneously, if they are in very close proximity, such as in an experimental playroom. Both of these options, however, have associated expenses. Numerous, experienced observers are both expensive and hard to come by. Further, repeated viewing of videotapes is very time consuming. It is often more time consuming to code videotapes of behavior than to code it live.

Scan sampling is less time consuming. In this procedure a whole group, such as a classroom, is sampled very rapidly at predetermined intervals. For example, to observe children's attention during various parts of the school day, one could utilize scan sampling. This involves observing separate individuals and recording their behavior instantaneously. It might take 60 seconds to record the attention of a classroom of 30 children. A number of separate scans would be conducted; the order in which each child is observed should vary across the relevant period. In this case, all observations would be aggregated for each child during that observation, creating one score. Separate scores for specific individuals taken within a short observational period, should not be treated as separate scores because they are not independent of each other (see the discussion of independence in Chapter 8). By aggregating across the individual observations, we get a whole (and reliable) picture of what individuals do during a certain period. By looking only at specific points, we only learn what they are doing at a specific instant.

Event or behavior sampling, as noted previously, involves choosing a specific event or behavior and recording it either continuously or as having occurred or not. This method is typically used in cases in which the target behavior does not occur with great frequency; therefore, one does not want to rely on time-oriented sampling because of the real risk of missing the behavior. Instead, the observer looks for the target behavior to occur and then records it. When recording an event, observers should make note of the specific endpoint, or consequence, of the behavior. Typically, an event recording is terminated when behaviors from another behavioral category begin. For, example, if we are observing aggression, we record those behaviors that comprise the category aggression. When the nature of the behavior changes, such as when one child comforts the other, the event recording should be terminated, but we should note that behavior that immediately succeeds the target behavior. These consequences of target behaviors, as noted in Chapter 5, provide insight into possible functions of the behavior.

Some basic sampling issues apply to behavioral sampling. As noted in the beginning of this section, sampling is an attempt to gather some information that is representative of larger bodies of information. To maximize the likelihood of gathering representative information, a few guidelines should be followed. First, one must observe the same individual at different points within the same day. By observing individuals at different points of the day we get a more representative picture. People do different things at 8 a.m. than they do at 2 p.m.! Similarly, by observing the same individual on different days we gain representativeness; Saturday morning child behavior is probably different from behavior on mornings that the child goes to school.

By extension, the specific order in which people are observed should be considered (e.g., counterbalanced or randomized) so that the order in which they are observed does not affect or confound our measures. In the case of counterbalancing we may have a total of 25 observational sampling slots in an observational period, say 1 per 30 seconds. Order of observation is counterbalanced when each child is observed in each of the 25 observational slots. So on day 1 John would be observed in slot 1 and Joan in slot 2. On day 2 John would be observed in slot 2 and Joan in slot 3, and so on. In the case of randomized order, the sampling slot (1–25) for each child on each day would be determined by randomly assigning the child to a slot. Thus, to ensure representative and nonconfounded data, the order in which we sample behavior should be either randomized or counterbalanced.

Recording Behavior

Specific recording rules correspond to certain sampling rules. This correspondence is displayed in Fig. 6.1. The quantitative measures that can be derived from each recording rule are displayed in Fig. 6.2.

Sampling Rules	Recording Rules		
	Continuous	0/1	Instantaneous
Ad Libitum			
Focal	X	X	X
Scan			X
Event	X	X	

FIG. 6.1. Sampling and recording rules.

Measures	Recording Rules		
	Continuous	*0/1*	*Instantaneous*
Frequency	X		
Duration	X		
Latency	X		
Pattern	X		
Intensity	X	X	X

FIG. 6.2.   Quantitative measures and recording rules.

Continuous recording rules can be used with focal person and event sampling strategies. With this form of recording, the observer records all behaviors of interest for the duration of the observational interval. In my R&T studies, I recorded continuously all social behavior and social interactants of the focal child for a full 3 minutes. The quantitative measures that can be derived from continuous recording are frequency, latency, duration, intensity, and pattern if the whole behavioral sequence of interest is observed during the specified interval. In addition to noting the behaviors of the focal child, it is useful to note during continuous recording the other children with whom the target child is interacting. For example, one could note the behaviors the focal child aims at other specific children and the behaviors others direct at the focal child.

Rather than coding behavior continuously across time, we might choose to sample discontinuously, or sample behavior at different time intervals. The recording rules based on time intervals include instantaneous sampling and 0/1 sampling. Before discussing these recording strategies, I diverge to discuss the choice of a sample interval (Martin & Bateson, 1993). By sample interval I mean the time interval used to determine the interval at which behavior is recorded. The observation period is divided into specific time intervals; the sample intervals are those points at which behavior is sampled. The point at the end of the sample interval is labeled the *sample point*.

Take the example of studying classroom attention. We could choose a sampling interval of 5, 10, 15, or more seconds in a 10-minute lesson. In the case of the 10-second interval in this lesson, we have a total of 60 sample points. Obviously, the shorter the duration the more the sample will resemble the universe of behavior and thus contain less error. Logistics of conducting observations, however, often limit short durations. For example, although we could have a 5-second sample interval to record classroom behavior if children are all seated, this short interval would be less practical if children were moving around the classroom or outdoors. Additionally, the degree of detail in a coding system affects the sample interval to the extent that more complex codes require more time than less complex codes. Finally, and as discussed in Chapter 8, repeated observations within a restricted time range bring into question the independence of the separate observations.

With all this in mind, I discuss the particulars of 0/1 and instantaneous sampling. With either of these methods, the observer should make clear the intervals at which behaviors are sampled. Although we may have a specific sampling interval, say 10 seconds, the exact moment at which we record the behavior may vary according to the rules followed. This section makes clear the way to explicate this process.

For simplicity's sake, let us say that our sample interval is 10 seconds. The observer would need some mechanical timer, such as a series of recorded beeps that the observer hears through an earphone, as a cue to record.

Beepers on digital watches are also useful but may be too loud for some locations, such as classrooms. With *instantaneous recording* (also called *point sampling*), the observer notes the occurrence or nonoccurrence or level of intensity of the behavior(s) of interest at the instant that the beeper goes off. Instantaneous recording is used with scan sampling. Complicated decisions about intensity ratings would impact on the sample interval; longer intervals are required for more complex ratings. Instantaneous recording can yield intensity scores. It can also yield scores that indicate the proportion of intervals during which specific behaviors were observed. It does not yield true frequencies because behavior is not being continuously recorded.

0/1 sampling (also labeled *interval sampling*) is similar to instantaneous sampling to the extent that a sample interval determines when we record. Unlike instantaneous sampling, however, 0/1 sampling simply records whether the behavior occurred (1) or didn't (0) during the whole 10-second interval, not at a specified instant. A behavior could have occurred only 1 time or as many as 10 times during the 10-second interval but a 1 would be scored in each instance. Like instantaneous sampling, 0/1 sampling can show the occurrence or nonoccurrence of behavior during a number of recording intervals. Consequentially, true frequency scores cannot be derived from 0/1 sampling. The advantage of 0/1 over instantaneous sampling is that is it easier for the observer, who has more time to process information in the former case. Indeed, if the sample interval is short enough, 0/1 and instantaneous sampling rules yield very similar measures (Smith, 1985).

SUMMARY AND CONCLUSIONS

In this chapter, I have outlined ways that observational categories can be sampled, recorded, and measured. The procedure that yields most information, focal child sampling with continuous recording, is also the most demanding in terms of time. Although other sampling and recording methods are less demanding, they have corresponding limitations in terms of the information yielded. Thus, it is imperative to determine what it is one wants to know and the types of measures necessary to answer that question. Based on that, an observer can choose sampling and recording strategies.

THINGS TO THINK ABOUT

1. Consider trying to measure the intensity of concentration. List some attributes by which you could measure intensity of local rate.

_____

_____

_____

_____

_____

_____

1a. Consider how intensity of concentration could be measured by consequence. Is there an independent measure of concentration that could guide your thinking?

_____

_____

_____

_____

_____

_____

2. Choose a situation in which to observe a group, say a classroom at recess or taking a test. Compare the information you get by using each of the sampling and corresponding recording techniques.

_____

_____

_____

3. List five things that would be most easily observed with event or behavior sampling.

4. List five things that could best be observed with scan sampling.

5. If you were interested in determining when during the school day children should be given recess, what sampling and recording methods could be used?

_____

_____

_____

_____

_____

_____

GLOSSARY

Actometer: A mechanical recording device, worn by participants, to measure physical activity.

Duration: A measure of time whereby an event or behavior is measured from beginning to end. For example, the duration of fantasy play bouts is 3 minutes.
Give your example:

_____

_____

_____

_____

Events: Behavioral episodes, contrasted with states, which are relatively short in duration. For example, hit is an event.
Give your example:

_____

_____

_____

_____

_____

Frequency: A measure of behavior that indicates the number of times the target behavior occurred within a specified time period. For example, there are 25 R&T bouts during a 30-minute recess period.

Give your example:

_____

_____

_____

_____

Intensity: A measure of behavior that indicates amplitude. For example, vigor of exercise can be scored along high, medium, and low dimensions.

Give your example:

_____

_____

_____

_____

Latency: A measure of time from the presentation of a stimulus to a reaction. For example, the latency is 3 seconds from when a teacher asked a question until he restated the question.

Give your example:

_____

_____

_____

_____

_____

Local rates: Applied to measuring intensity and are measured by noting the number of behavioral components that occur with a specific duration. For example, if 5 out of 8 components of R&T are exhibited during a 5-minute interval.
Give your example:

_____

_____

_____

_____

_____

Measurement: Quantification of behavioral units, typically expressed in terms of frequency, duration, intensity, pattern, and latency.
Give your example:

_____

_____

_____

_____

_____

Pattern: A measure of behavior that describes the way in which different types of behavior are patterned, or occur, across time. For example, when presented with a new toy, children will exhibit the following pattern: exploration, play, boredom.
Give your examples:

_____

_____

_____

Recording, 0/1: Recording behavior that occurs during a specified time interval. For example, record occurrence of a smile if it occurs during a 30-second interval.
   Give your example:

_____

_____

_____

_____

Recording, continuous: Recording all behaviors that occur during a specified interval. For example, record all the relevant behaviors of a child for 3 minutes.
   Give your example:

_____

_____

_____

_____

Recording, instantaneous: Recording behaviors that occur at a specified instant. For example, score occurrence only if it is observed when a beeper sounds.
   Give your examples:

_____

_____

_____

_____

Sample interval: Those time units into which the observational session is divided. For example, a 15-minute lesson could be divided into fifteen 1-minute intervals.
Give your example:

_____

_____

_____

_____

_____

Sample point: That point at the end of the sample interval.
Give your example:

_____

_____

_____

_____

_____

Sampling, ad lib: Sampling behavior in such a way that no systematic rules are being followed.
Give your example:

_____

_____

_____

_____

_____

Sampling, behavior/event: Observing specified sets of behaviors or events; contrasted with time sampling. For example, record all instances of aggression.
Give your example:

_____

_____

_____

_____

_____

Sampling, focal child: Sampling the behavior of individual children separately.
Give your example:

_____

_____

_____

_____

_____

Sampling, scan: Sampling whole groups by briefly observing individuals within the group at short intervals.
Give your example:

_____

_____

_____

_____

Sampling, time: Choosing to observe based on specified time intervals; in contrast to behavior/event sampling. For example, record behavior every 20 seconds.
Give your example:

_____

_____

_____

_____

_____

States: Behavioral episodes, contrasted with events, which are relatively long in duration. For example, fighting is a state.
Give your example:

_____

_____

_____

_____

_____

Vigor: An intensity measure of physical activity. For example, higher heart rate is a measure of vigor.
Give your example:

_____

_____

_____

_____

_____

7

Reliability and Validity

In this chapter, I discuss two technical aspects of measurement and then discuss them in terms of behavioral observational measurement. These technical aspects are reliability and validity. By reliability I mean the consistency of a measure. Validity, on the other hand, is concerned with the extent to which a measure actually measures what it says it measures. Resounding the well-known saw: Reliability is necessary but not sufficient for validity. In this chapter, I discuss some of the assumptions behind reliability and validity and ways in which we can maximize them in observational work. Because reliability and validity issues are explicitly tied to the ways in which we categorize and measure behavior, the discussion in this chapter is relevant to discussions of category definition and measurement. Thus, Chapters 5, 6, and 7 should be used in concert.

My discussion of reliability and validity is centered on category formation and measurement. Consequently, I will not be covering the statistical dimensions of reliability and validity at more than a superficial level. Students interested in more detailed discussion of the statistical bases of reliability and validity of observational measures are referred other excellent source books (Bakeman & Gottman, 1986; Suen & Ary, 1989). Students not interested in the more technical aspects of reliability and validity are advised to skim the sections on statistics and the validity sections on signs and samples and different forms of validity.

A basic assumption I follow throughout this chapter is that reliability and validity are not properties of any one instrument or behavioral category embedded in an instrument (Herbert & Attridge, 1975; Suen & Ary, 1989). Rather, reliability and validity are properties of the outcomes of an instrument; that is, reliability and validity are derived from the measures or scores resulting from the processes of categorization, sampling, and recording behavior. As was discussed in the preceding chapters, a number of factors external to the instrument itself, affect the accuracy of behavioral recording, for instance, poor visibility or fatigued observers. With these qualifiers and assumptions stated, I discuss, in order, reliability and then validity of behavioral measures.

RELIABILITY

Reliability of observational measures is judged in terms of consistency. Consistency as I use it has two dimensions: consistency within an individual observer and consistency among multiple observers. Most simply put, consistency means that one person describes the same thing across time and different people describe the same behaviors in the same way. Take for example a case of a father and son sitting on the floor, each coloring a separate picture. As an observer I am concerned with affect displays, such as *smile, laugh, frown,* and *cry.* Consistency within an observer, or intraobserver reliability, applied to this scenario involves assessing the degree to which one observer consistently, across time, scored the same behaviors in the same categories. A particular set of facial expressions, then, should consistently be assigned to one of the four categories.

Consistency between observers, or interobserver reliability, is a measure of the degree to which different people simultaneously assign specific behaviors to specific categories. Obviously intraobserver reliability is necessary in cases with either one or more than one observer: If there is no internal consistency there cannot be consistency among individuals! More is said about these two forms of reliability later in this chapter.

Reliability at What Level?

When deciding on a reliability procedure, a most basic question to be asked is: At what level should the observer(s) be agreeing? The level to which I refer is the level of detail in the behavioral units considered (Sackett, 1978; Suen & Ary, 1989). Take the example of the father and son coloring. The unit of analysis for documenting reliability should be the same as the unit of analysis as specified by our theory and measures used for subsequent data analyses. If our theory of affect and our data analysis plans (which are realized in the Results section of a research report) conceptualize affect in terms of the four levels of facial expression, then reliability should be established at that level, not at a more microlevel (e.g., different dimensions of smile) or at a more macrolevel (e.g., positive and negative affect).

With this basic consideration in mind, two factors in addition to consistency determine how reliable measures are: *sensitivity* and *resolution* (Martin & Bateson, 1993). Sensitivity can be judged by investigating the degree to which actual changes in behavior are reflected in the measured values. For example, to what degree do our scores show sensitivity to changes in facial expression? Resolution concerns the degree of change in behavior and how it is reflected in the scoring. More simply, resolution concerns the smallest change that can be detected in the true value of the behavior. Resolution in this example refers to the dimensions of smile and laugh that can be detected. All these factors affect intraobserver and interobserver reliability.

Intraobserver Reliability

Intraobserver reliability refers to the degree of consistency with which one observer repeatedly observes and scores the behavior across time. The same behavior could be recorded with a video camera and viewed by an observer on separate occasions. Alternatively, one observer could observe the same behavior in the same individual across time, say at different points in one session. Additionally, the observer could observe the same behavior in different individuals across time. The degree of intraobserver reliability is expressed numerically as the agreement between the two sets of scores. Although there are a variety of statistical techniques to address this issue, such as Cronbach's generalizability theory (Cronbach, Gleser, Nanda, & Rajaratnam, 1972) and classical theory, all scores basically tell the extent to which one individual's scores are consistent. In the remainder of this section, I address some for the simpler techniques of expressing reliability.

The degree to which two sets of observations by the same observer are reliable can be conceptualized in ways similar to those that are used to determine the reliability of tests. Indeed, the statistical procedures for measuring intraobserver reliability are derived from various test reliability theories. Here I discuss two techniques derived from classical theory, *test–retest reliability* and *split-half reliability* (See Bakeman & Gottman, 1986, and Suen & Ary, 1989 for more detailed discussions). Test–retest reliability is an indicator of the stability of a score from time 1 to time 2. The degree to which the same score occurs across time is the measure of test–retest reliability.

The same logic and statistics can be applied to repeated observations by the same person. In the example of affect, say that the observations were videotaped so we could determine the degree to which a single observer coded the same behavior, such as *smile*, across two separate viewings of 10 separate sessions. Table 7.1 displays the match or mismatch between two separate codings. The X indicates that a smile was scored and a O indicates that one was not. A + in the last column indicates between session agreement and – indicates disagreement.

We could treat, by analogy, the two coding sessions as two testing sessions and the separate sessions as items in the tests. Intraobserver reliability is measured by

TABLE 7.1
Intraobserver Reliability of Two Recodings Across 10 Sessions

Session	Coding 1	Coding 2	Agree/Disagree
1	X	X	+
2	X	O	–
3	X	X	+
4	O	X	–
5	X	X	+
6	O	O	+
7	O	O	+
8	X	X	+
9	X	X	+
10	O	O	+

determining the extent to which the separate testings or observations yield the same scores. We sample across 10 different observations, rather than choosing just one observation point. For sampling-related reasons, more samples yield a more accurate picture of the universe of behaviors.

There are various statistical techniques that could be applied to these data to generate intraobserver reliability coefficients. I name and briefly discuss them here. In Chapter 9, I outline the way in which the statistics are calculated. Most simply, an *index of concordance* (Martin & Batseon, 1993) or a percentage of agreement can be calculated. This statistic is calculated as:

$$Sum +/Sum + -$$

In this case we have 8/8 + 2 or 80%. If you choose to use .80 instead of 80%, you should note explicitly somewhere in the report that the measure is a percent measure, not a correlation coefficient or a kappa coefficient.

Although the use of percentage of agreement has been roundly criticized on a number of grounds, such as failure to correct for chance agreements, the influence of the number of codes, and the inability to compare percentages of agreement to any criterion, it is still useful at a simple level: It gives us a rough and ready indicator of agreement. Like all measures of percentage, scores range from 0 to 100.

Other measures of reliability applicable to test–retest data are different correlation coefficients, such as the Pearson r or Spearman's rho. Although both of these techniques are discussed Chapter 9, I briefly explain their meaning here. Both correlation coefficients are represented with r; the Spearman coefficient is sometimes represented as rs. Basically, correlations coefficients tell us the degree to which two sets of measures, like the 10 sessions coded on two occasions, co-occur. Perfect co-occurrences are expressed as +1.0 and –1.0: Correlation coefficients range from –1.0 to +1.0. A less than perfect correlation coefficient is .65. Positive correlations indicate that as we observe one measure, such as smiling in a father, we also observe another measures, such as smiling in a son. A negative correlation, on the other hand, indicates that as one behavior is observed with increasing frequency, another is observed with decreasing frequency. Correlation coefficients, unlike percentages of agreement, have the added benefit of telling us the degree to which a particular coefficient is due to chance. In short, with correlations coefficients we also can determine a p value or probability statement. We can determine that when $r = .65$ with a sample of 10, the probability of getting this finding by chance is .05. We can thus be sure that in 95 of 100 cases, if we were to take a similar sample, we would get an r of .65.

Whereas test–retest reliability is a measure of stability, split-half reliability is a measure of homogeneity. Rather than measuring across different observation sessions, we measure within a session. The information presented in Table 7.1 can be used to illustrate the point. Look at one individual coding 10 separate sessions (listed in the Coding 1 column) for smile. The X on each line represents a hit, that is, scoring a smile when one actually occurred. The O represents a miss, or coding a smile when one did not occur or not coding a smile when one did occur. Split-half reliability can be calculated by comparing scores from odd items (in this case, sessions 1, 3, 5, 7, and 9) with those from even items (2, 4, 6, 8, and 10) or comparing the first 5 sessions with the second 5 sessions. Correlation coefficients between the two sets of scores are then calculated. The degree to which the two sets of scores co-occur ranges from +1.0 to –1.0.

To conclude this section, intraobserver reliability is a measure of the degree to which an individual observer is consistent. Consistency can be considered in terms of repeated scorings of the same events or of different scorings across time. Consistency of an individual observer is necessary in cases involving one or more observers. We want to make sure that each individual is consistent.

It has been suggested (Martin & Bateson, 1993) that adding a measure of interobserver reliability is valuable to the extent that it guards against only one person seeing the world in a particular way, albeit a consistently particular way. In the next section I address interobserver reliability.

Interobserver Reliability

Whereas intraobserver reliability is a measure of consistency within an individual, *interobserver reliability* is a measure of consistency between observers. Like the within-individual case, interobserver reliability can be determined by videotaping (or audiorecording for oral language data) relevant behavior and measuring the degree to which more than one person agrees on the scoring of a particular behavior or set of behaviors. Alternatively, two or more observers can score the same sessions live and simultaneously.

Establishing interobserver reliability is a 2-stage process. First, *intraobserver* reliability should be established. Being assured that each observer is consistent in his or her observations is obviously necessary before more than one observer can agree. Second, different observers must be chosen in order to check the degree to which they agree on what they describe. Procedurally, this usually involves external observers checking a set number of observers who are collecting the data or the primary observers checking themselves. In the former case, one or more observers who are not the primary data collectors can check on the observations of the primary observers by simultaneously observing the same phenomena or by recoding sets of tapes and then comparing codes. In the case of primary observers checking each other, observers could be assigned to recode (on video or audiotape) the codes of another observer. In either case, the reliability checks are conducted on a sample of the total observations.

When some form of time sampling is used, it is necessary that both observers are coding at exactly the same time. To this end, it is necessary that observers simultaneously receive an external signal, such as a beep, so that they are coding at the same time. In areas where quiet is necessary, such as in a classroom or in an observation booth, it is best to have a prerecorded tape, with a series of timed beeps. Each observer could have an earphone attached to a recorder playing the tape of programmed beeps. In areas where quiet is not important, the earphone is not necessary and the prerecorded tape could play aloud. Alternatively, the countdown beepers common on so many inexpensive digital watches do very nicely.

It is often best that checks are made on a random sample of data. In this way representativeness of the sample is assured. For example, in some of my studies I have observers check the codes on 20% of all the codes. The original codes are then compared with the recodings.

A variety of different statistical procedures have been developed to gauge the degree to which different observers agree with each other. In this section, I discuss some of the more common strategies for calculating interobserver reliability (Suen & Ary, 1989) such as the smaller/larger index, the percentage of agreement, the occurrence/nonoccurrence agreement index, and kappa. For a more thorough treatment of the various statistical procedures, see Suen and Ary (1989). I begin with a very simple procedure, the *smaller/larger index* (S/L). This procedure can be used when two observers code the same behavior, for example, smiles. Take the example of one observer coding a child smiling 25 times and another coding the same child as smiling 32 times. The S/L is calculated by dividing the smaller value by the larger value:

$$\frac{S}{L} = \frac{smaller}{larger}$$
$$\frac{S}{L} = \frac{25}{32}$$
$$\frac{S}{L} = .78$$

The S/L index is simple but has been criticized in terms of its inability to address the degree to which two observers actually agreed on the behaviors. Even if each observer scored 32 cases of smiling in the previous case and a perfect index of 1.0 was derived, we would not be sure that the two observers scored the same 32 smiles. We only know that they scored the same number.

The second technique for calculating interobserver reliability is the *percentage of agreement*. With this procedure, two observers code the same behaviors, and then their codes are compared. This procedure was discussed in the section on intraobserver reliability so I do not spend much time on it here. Suffice it to say that the percentage of agreement statistic, although widely used, has been criticized on grounds that it does not correct for agreements due to chance (Bakeman & Gottman, 1986; Suen & Ary, 1989). In cases of extremely frequently occurring and extremely infrequently occurring behaviors, the probability of chance agreement is inflated (Suen & Ary, 1989). In other words, when behaviors occur very frequently or very infrequently, the percentage of agreement statistic is influenced by observers agreeing due to chance, not necessarily due to their coding the same thing.

It is a useful exercise when examining the percentage of agreement to generate an agreement or confusion matrix (Bakeman & Gottman, 1986) to see the specific behaviors that are the most agreed on as well as those that are not agreed upon. Such a matrix for two observers coding the following behaviors is displayed in Fig. 7.1: smile, laugh, frown, and cry.

A useful aspect of this matrix is that we can spot those areas in which observers agree and those in which they disagree. Those areas of agreement between the two observers lie along the diagonal from smile to cry. The areas outside of this diagonal show disagreement. Thus, there was frequent disagreement between the observers on laugh

	Smile	Laugh	Frown	Cry	Total
			Observer 1		
Observer 2					
Smile	15	12	0	0	27
Laugh	18	13	0	0	31
Frown	0	0	22	2	24
Cry	0	1	1	16	18
Total	33	26	23	18	100

FIG. 7.1.   Confusion matrix.

and cry. This information is useful for training observers to become more reliable in areas that are problematic.

The next procedure to express interobserver reliability, the *occurrence and nonoccurrence indices of agreement,* takes into account the frequency with which a behavior occurs (Suen & Ary, 1989). The occurrence index is calculated by dividing the occurrence of agreements by the occurrence of agreements plus disagreements and multiplying by 100%. This statistic is graphically represented as

$$\%oa = \text{occurrence of agree}$$
$$= \text{occurrence agree + disagree x 100\%}$$

By contrast, nonoccurrence agreement is calculated by dividing the total of nonagreements by the total of nonagreements plus agreements and multiplying by 100%. This can be represented as

$$\%nona = \text{nonoccurrence agreement}$$
$$= \text{nonoccurrence agreement + agree x 100\%.}$$

The occurrence and nonoccurrence indices reduce chance agreement due to frequently and infrequently observed behaviors, respectively. Thus, separate indices should be used with different types of behavior. The occurrence index can be used when a behavior occurs at levels of 80% or above whereas the nonoccurrence index can be used when behaviors are at 20% or below (Suen & Ary, 1989). An example is presented in Fig. 7.2.

Let us say that two observers are coding, simultaneously, occurrence or nonoccurrence of mutual gaze by a mother and her son. For the occurrence index, we see that the two observers agreed three times (at intervals 1, 3, and 5) and disagreed four times (at intervals 4, 7, 9, and 10). Taking these data and applying them to the occurrence agreement formula (%oa) we get

$$\frac{3}{3 + 4 \times 100\%} = 42.8\%$$

Observer 1	1	0	1	1	1	0	1	0	0	1
Observer 2	1	0	1	0	1	0	0	0	1	0
Interval	1	2	3	4	5	6	7	8	9	10

FIG. 7.2   Occurrence (1)/nonoccurrence (O) codes between two observers.

For the nonoccurrence formula, %nona, we have 3 agreements for nonoccurrence (at intervals 2, 6, and 8) and 4 disagreements, resulting in

$$\frac{3}{3 + 4} \times 100\% = 42.8\%$$

The next interobserver statistic to be discussed is kappa. Kappa is a frequently recommended statistic (e.g., Bakeman & Gottman, 1986; Suen & Ary, 1989) because it accounts for chance agreements more completely than the previous procedure. The equation for kappa (k; Cohen, 1960, as cited in Suen & Ary, 1989) is expressed as:

$$k = \frac{po - pe}{1 - pe}$$

where po is the proportion of agreement and pe is the expected proportion of agreement.

The data presented in Fig. 7.2 serve as an illustration. Figure 7.3 shows a 2x2 matrix that provides a tally for occurrences and nonoccurrences for the two observers (Suen & Ary, 1989). The matrix is completed by entering in cell b the proportion of intervals for which both observers agreed on occurrence (i.e., 3:10 or .3), in cell c the proportion of intervals for which both observers agreed on nonoccurrence (i.e., 3:10 or .3), in cell a the proportion of intervals where Observer 1 scored occurrences and Observer 2 scored nonoccurrences (i.e., 3:10, or .30), and in cell d the proportion of intervals where Observer 1 reported nonoccurrence and Observer 2 reported occurrence (i.e., 1:10 or .10). The margins, or p1, p2, q1, and q2, are the sums of their respective rows and columns. To calculate po, in the kappa formula we add cells b + c (i.e., .30 + .30 = .60). Thus, po = .60. pe is calculated by multiplying

			Observer 1		
		Nonoccurrence		*Occurrence*	
Occurrence	(a)	.30	(b)	.30	.60
			Observer 2		
Nonoccurrence	(c)	.30	(d)	.10	.40
	(q2)	.60	(p2)	.40	1.0

FIG. 7.3.   Occurrence–nonoccurrence matrix for two observers.

p1 by p2, multiplying q1 by q2, and adding the two products. To calculate k, the formula

$$k = \frac{b + c - p1p2 - q1q2}{1 - p1p2 - q1q2}$$

is used, yielding

$$k = \frac{(.30 + .30) - (.24 - .24)}{1 - (.24 - .24)}$$

or

$$k = \frac{.60 - (0)}{1 - (0)}$$

or $k = .60$. Kappa coefficients, like correlation coefficients, range from -1.0 to $+1.0$, where the former indicates that observers agree completely and the latter indicates that they disagree totally. Any negative kappa indicates that observers agree at a less than chance level. A kappa of .60 is considered acceptable, whereas a kappa of .80 or above is good (Suen & Ary, 1989).

To summarize, reliability can be considered at two levels, intraobserver and interobserver reliability. Both of the terms relate to the degree of consistency within and between observers, or the degree to which observers see the same thing consistently. There are various statistical procedures that allow us to gauge the level of consistency. The standards vary against which reliability statistics are compared. For the S/L index, percentage of agreement, and occurrence–nonoccurrence statistics, no standard exists. For correlation and kappa coefficients we have probability statements associated with the reliability statistics so that we know the probability of getting a particular statistic by chance. Kappa has the added benefit of accounting for chance agreement between observers. All these factors converge to the point that kappa is the recommended reliability statistic. Although the calculations of kappa may be bothersome, numerous statistical packages available for both microcomputers and mechanical recording devices calculate kappa as part of their data analysis packages.

Factors Affecting Reliability

Just as the statistical technique can affect the reliability statistic that is generated, other factors can affect the reliability of the observations themselves. I discussed the extent to which behaviors that occur very frequently or infrequently can affect reliability. I have noted that high and low frequency behaviors are susceptible to chance agreement and consequently artificially inflate reliability. In this final section on reliability, I address three other factors that have an impact on reliability. They are observer fatigue, category definition, and observer drift (Martin & Bateson, 1993).

Observer fatigue occurs during long and sometimes monotonous observation periods. It results in observers not attending fully to the behavior; consequently, unreliable data are collected. Three possible remedies are available. First, the length of the observation session could be shortened so that within-session fatigue and boredom are minimized. A second solution, where multiple observers are available, is to rotate observers through a variety of observational time slots and contexts. Indeed, counterbalancing observers in this way is a necessary safeguard against confounding a specific observer with a specific data set. If only one observer records the behavior of one particular group or during one time period, then the data from that group and time period may be idiosyncratic to that one observer. Thus, counterbalancing multiple observers avoids a number of problems.

A third way of addressing the problem of observer fatigue is for observers to record the behaviors in the field with a video camera and then code the recording later. Although the use of videotape recorders and other mechanical recording devices is no panacea (see Chapter 10), some problems are alleviated by their use.

The second and related reliability issue is *observer drift.* By observer drift I mean that observers in the course of a study code the same behaviors in different ways. Observer drift typically rears its ugly head in protracted studies, where coding goes on across a long period of time. For example, an experimenter observing children's playground behavior across the school year. At the beginning of the year, he or she trains observers to meet a specific reliability criterion for each behavior. Observer drift occurs when, with the passage of time, observers change how they code specific behaviors. They may have started off coding mutual gaze between two children as social interaction but one month later code the same behavior as nonsocial behavior. They may have implicitly changed their criterion for social interaction to include verbal exchanges only.

To guard against observer drift requires that observers are monitored and retrained. More specifically, in cases of prolonged studies, interobserver checks should be made at various points throughout the study, say every two weeks or every month. Furthermore, periodic retraining is also necessary. In our studies of school recess, for example, observers were retrained in coding videotapes of recess behavior every two months.

The third factor affecting reliability is *category definition.* Clearly defined categories are more reliable than ambiguous categories. As I noted in Chapter 5, molecular-level categories are generally more reliable than molar-level categories. So for example, smile is more reliably coded than happy. Molar categories can be used, but they should be described to observers in terms of their specific components. It is often helpful to define a category in terms of core dimensions and borderline dimensions. For example, in the category rough-and-tumble play, we might consider hit, kick to be core dimension in that they represent the basis of what we consider our category to represent. In this case the core is considered play fighting. Borderline dimensions, on the other hand, belong to the category, but their inclusion is less crucial to the definition of the category. In the rough-and-tumble play example, chase may be considered a borderline dimension in that we consider nonrough though physically vigorous behaviors to be part of the category but not at the heart of it. It is obviously important to decide, in advance, the extent to which observers will include instances of borderline cases.

To summarize this discussion of reliability, I suggest that vigilance is necessary to guard against unreliable or inconsistent observations. If our observations are unreliable, they are useless!

VALIDITY

In this section I discuss validity. By *validity,* I mean most generally truthfulness. Most simply, a measure is valid if we use it to describe what we say we are describing. The simplicity of this definition is deceptive, however, because validity can be very elusive. The truthfulness of a statement depends on one's theory and the social context in which the validity question is posed. Different theories may define constructs differently; thus, each theory may have a different definition of a specific category. For example, some theories define rough-and-tumble play in terms of play fighting, whereas others consider it part of the category aggression.

The social context in which validity is established also has an impact on its definition. In the field of assessment of children in schools, for example, some educators are insisting that the impact of the assessment information on the educational system should be considered in the validity decisions (Moss, 1992). In considering the validity of a specific assessment program, whether the program is based on tests or observations, consideration should be given to the consequences of the assessment: Do such assessments raise children's level of anxiety.

These are but two very general theoretical and policy issues that impact on validity. In the remainder of this chapter, I concentrate on the technical factors that impact on validity.

At the beginning of this chapter, I discussed reliability as necessary but not sufficient for validity. This means that we must see things consistently before we can say anything about them, and even then, there is a question of truthfulness. For example, two people may be observing a child simultaneously and not agree on the extent to which the child is active (i.e., interobserver reliability). What is are the implications of this for the truthfulness of the conclusions about the child ? These observers may have intraobserver reliability, but they do not have interobserver reliability and so do not have validity.

Moreover, consistency alone (i.e., reliability) is not sufficient for validity. For example, I teach an undergraduate course in child study. In that course I give two examinations to measure the extent to which the students understand children and ways of looking at them. Thus, the validity of the exams relates to the specific issues we covered in class and in assignments. For the sake of illustration, let us say that each exam contains 20 multiple choice items on single digit multiplication. These exams should be very reliable to the extent that they should exhibit a high degree of test–retest reliability and intrascorer and interscorer reliability. Even though these two tests are reliable, they are obviously not valid. To establish validity requires something more than just reliability, although reliability is a necessary starting point.

Validity, unlike reliability, cannot be measured directly (Suen & Ary, 1989). Rather, validity coefficients tell us the degree to which our behavioral measures, say of playfulness, relate to other (theoretically related) measures, such as other measures of playfulness. As such, validity involves making a theoretical connection among different sets of variables, some observable and others not observable. For example, playfulness is an unobservable, inferential construct; consequentially, the validity of a playfulness measure should be more difficult to establish than that of an observable set of behaviors, such as rough-and-tumble play. This very simple example of validity should be the basis on which to understand the varied forms of validity discussed in subsequent sections of this chapter.

Validity: High and Low Inference and Molar and Molecular Categories

The distinction between categories involving high levels of inference and categories involving low levels of inference becomes important in a discussion of validity. This section is a very detailed discussion of ways to establish validity for these two types of categories and can be read in two different ways. For a person interested in fine-tuned distinctions between different levels of category inference, the section should be read carefully. For those interested in a general distinction between high and low inference categories, the section can be read less systematically. General comment sections at the end of relevant paragraphs provide summaries.

Unobservable constructs, such as romance, have been labeled *signs* by Suen and Ary (1989). They are theoretical categories, and a sign represents them. Thus, signs are high inference. A *sample,* on the other hand, is low inference and can be observed directly. Samples include such things as smile, kiss, and hug. (Sample, as used here to refer to types of category, should not be confused with use of sampling techniques discussed in preceding chapters.) High inference and low inference categories, in turn, can be measured through the use of molecular and molar categories (Suen & Ary, 1989). Molecular measures are usually at a physical level of description and involve a single observable behavior, such as push. Molar measures, on the other hand, represent an aggregate of subcomponents; for example, R&T can be a molar category that is the aggregate of a number of molecular measures such as hit, push, smile, and so on.

It is useful to think of the validity of observational data when they are conceptualized along the dimensions of molar–molecular and high–low inference. The dimensions are displayed in Fig. 7.4.

Behaviors can be assigned along four dimensions, corresponding to the cells in this matrix. Cell 1 is a molecular–low inference measure; for playfulness this might include hit-at and open hand. Molecular–low inference measures have been considered, on face value, valid to the extent that little inference about the meaning of the behavior is needed: Hit-at and open hand simply represent what they say they represent.

Cell 3 includes molar–low inference measures, aggregates of observable subcomponents. R&T is a molar sample behavior it is the aggregate of the molecular sample behaviors. Validity of this measure, or the extent to which it really represents the category R&T, can be derived from the theoretical and empirical literature. For

	Low	High
Molecular	1	2
Molar	3	4

FIG. 7.4   High–low inference x molecular–molar measures.

example, to what degree does extant theory suggest that the behaviors listed represent something called R&T? The degree to which these behaviors come together into a homogeneous category called R&T can be established through techniques such as factor analysis.

General comments: Validity of low inference categories is established by considering the extent to which each behavioral component of a category and their aggregate are theoretically consistent with the conceptualization of the category.

For more inferential categories, consider sign-level measures. Recall sign-level categories are unobservable. Working with romance as an example of a sign category, we can say that cell 2, molecular–high inference, is affect. In cell 4, molar–high inference, is an aggregate of the molecular sign behaviors comprising cell 3.

General comments: High inference categories, like low inference categories, are formed by noting individual components (molecular) and aggregating them into a molar category. The difference between high and low inference categories is the degree to which each is directly observable.

The different levels of inference for these categories require different validity decisions for each cell and for each of the different types of validity. In the next section, I address briefly the common dimensions of validity. Additionally, I outline the conditions necessary for validity for several types of validity.

Validity: Different Forms

In this section, I discuss three types of validity: construct, content, and criterion-related. These three different forms of validity, when used in schools, they have recently been discussed in terms of policy implications (Moss, 1992). For the sake of clarity, they are discussed separately. However, the different forms of validity are interrelated and taken together tell us something about what we are measuring. Indeed, recent conceptualizations of validity are that it is a unitary (not trinity) construct, with construct validity at its heart (Linn, 1994).

Construct validity is considered to be the most basic form of validity to which all measures should aspire (Linn, 1994; Loevenger, 1957; Messick, 1975, 1983; Moss, 1992). Construct validity refers to, the degree to which the behaviors measured represent a theoretical construct; constructs, by definition, are not observable and thus high inference. Construct validity is closely tied to a theory of whatever we are trying to measure.

General comment: If we are not concerned with measuring a construct, such as when we use molar and molecular sample measures, construct validity should not a concern (Suen & Ary, 1989).

When high inference measures are used, however, construct validity is very important because we are purporting to measure something abstract. With each type of high inference measure, molar and molecular, we must address the extent to which our categories reflect what we say they reflect. This is the construct validity question. Construct validity is traditionally established by correlating the behavioral measure with other theoretically relevant measures. A behavioral measure should correlate positively with measures of a similar construct (i.e., convergent validity) and negatively or not all with some measures (i.e., discriminant validity). For example, the behavioral components of romance should relate positively to related measures, such as positive affect displays, and negatively to measures of inhibition.

General comment: For molecular–high inference measures, construct validity simply means correlating that one high inference measure (recall molecular measures have only one component) with another, theoretically related measure (Suen & Ary, 1989). For molar–high inference measures, however, two processes are necessary to establish construct validity. First, the molecular components of the molar category should be homogeneous, or internally consistent. Establishing internal consistency can be accomplished through a number of statistical routines, such as factor analyses and generalizability theory. These procedures are beyond the scope of this book and the interested reader is referred to Suen and Ary (1989) for a detailed and very clearly presented technical discussion. Second, each of the components of the molar category, and the molar category as a whole should be related to other measures purported to measure that construct. The empirical relations between measures is tested with correlation coefficients.

Content validity is a measure of the degree to which a specific measure represents the components of the variable being measured. Content validity can be best understood if we begin by talking about the content validity of tests and then move to observational data. Content validity of a test is established by measuring the degree to which the test measures what was taught (see Pellegrini, 1992 for a thorough description of validity and tests). The components of the variable of interest (i.e., what was taught) are represented by the instructional objectives for the class taking the test. Content validity is determined by the match or mismatch between the test items and the instructional objectives. An instrument is content valid if it measures the same material that is taught.

For observational data, I address the content validity for the four levels of categories displayed in Fig. 7.3. For molecular–low inference measures, the measures themselves represent the domain; as with construct validity, molecular–low inference measures are content valid by definition. If we take the measure hit-at/open, this measure represents that domain.

For molar–high inference measures, on the other hand, no single sign can represent the whole domain in which one is interested; molar-high inference measures cannot be content valid (Suen & Ary, 1989). Therefore, hit-at/open cannot represent the domain of R&T because R&T has many more components. Because molar–low inference measures are aggregates of subcomponents, to establish content validity we must establish the content validity of each molecular–low inference behavior first. Then we must judge the degree to which all the molecular–low inference measures taken together represent the domain in which we are interested. For example, to establish the content validity of R&T here we must be assured that our molecular samples are representative of R&T. Thus, we should have components that relate the three definitive dimensions of play: affect, such as smiling; vigor, such as run and hit; and structure, such as top and bottom positions in wrestling. As with content validity in tests, we must judge the degree to which measures actually represent a domain.

One way of establishing this is to ask a panel of experts to list the dimensions and gauge the degree to which the dimensions match.

Finally, we have the high inference–molar categories. To establish content validity in these cases, we use all the procedures utilized to establish content validity for molar–low inference measures.

General comment: Low inference molecular measures are content valid by definition. The aggregate of low inference measures is determined by the extent to which theory or experts consider them a category. Molecular–high inference categories, on the other hand, cannot be content valid because no one high inference measure can represent a larger category and a molar.

The final type of validity, *criterion-related validity,* has two components: *predictive validity* and *concurrent validity.* In both cases we relate a behavioral measure to some other criterion. The difference between concurrent and predictive validity is one of time. In the case of concurrent validity, two measures (one of which is our observational measure) are taken at roughly the same time. In predictive validity, the observational measure is taken at one time and another measure is taken at another time. To gauge each form of criterion validity, correlation coefficients are used. The magnitude of the correlation between R&T at time 1 and social role taking at time 2, for example $r = .30$, tells us the degree to which R&T is predictive of social role taking. The fact that R&T is predictive in this way suggests that the R&T measure is picking up something useful in that it relates systematically to other measures.

If we think that R&T is a dimension of play, we can correlate it with another contemporaneous measure of play, such as fantasy. The degree to which the two measures are intercorrelated is the index of concurrent validity.

General comments: Molecular–low inference criterion validity is simply a measure of observer accuracy (Suen & Ary, 1989). Alternatively, for either molecular–high inference or molar–high inference measures we simply correlate our observational measures at each of these levels and then correlate them with the behavioral measures of those variables. We may also correlate them with other types of measures, such as questionnaires. For example, R&T may correlate with other behavioral measures of vigorous behavior, such as chasing, with a teacher questionnaire that rates children's engagement in different forms of activities, including R&T.

Threats to Validity

Earlier in this chapter, I outlined some threats to the reliability of observational measures. As reliability and validity are linked, those threats to reliability are also threats to validity. Two additional threats specific to validity are reactivity and observer bias. Because these issues were discussed extensively in Chapter 3, I only touch on them here.

Reactivity refers to the extent to which the subjects of observations act differently simply because they know we are observing them. For example, if we are observing mothers reading to children, mothers could act unnaturally or act the way they think observers think they should be acting (see Sears, Maccoby, & Levin, 1957). Thus, the validity issue here is concerned with the truthfulness of our observations as representations of mother–child interaction. Observers could be 100% consistent in their codings but still not address the validity issue. There are numerous ways to minimize this problem, but probably the surest method involves repeated and lengthy observations. As participants habituate to being observed, they act more natural.

The issue of *observer bias,* too, is important. Recall that observer bias exists when observers tend to see what they want to see. In Chapter 3, I gave a number of examples of observers who were aware of the hypotheses of the study and of the experimental conditions to which children were assigned and coded observational data in ways consistent with the research hypotheses. Interobserver reliability was high in all these studies, but they were all reliably biased. A safeguard against bias is to use blind and double blind procedures. For example, we should have observers unaware of the hypotheses of the study and, if relevant, to children's groups assignment. Furthermore, if children are also given tests, interviews, or question-naires, observers should be blind to the results, which may bias subsequent obser-vations of the children. For example, if the same person interviewed a child and the results of that interview suggested that he or she was aggressive, that knowledge would probably influence subsequent observations. In observing ambiguous cases, such as making distinctions between R&T and aggression, observer bias may lead the observer to code the child's behavior as aggressive. It also makes sense, where a number of observers are available, to counterbalance observers across sessions and children. That is, different observers should observe different children and conduct observations at different times.

SUMMARY AND CONCLUSIONS

In this chapter, I discussed two technical dimensions of conducting behavioral observations: reliability and validity. These are both very important to the degree that we should agree on what we see (i.e., reliability) and that we are measuring what we say we are measuring (i.e., validity). With both of these conditions met, however, we still have no guarantee that our measures are really valid. Validity, as I noted, is a very subjective business. Our conceptualizations of validity for a specific construct may, for example, be representative of only one theoretical position, and that position in turn may be questionable. In short, we should recognize that we are making reasonable guesses about validity, and we should be open to the vagaries involved such that we are willing to incorporate new dimen-sions of a construct into our models.

A good example of the ways in which notions of validity change is the current discussion of validity and testing in school settings (Moss, 1992). High stakes testing is an area of real concern is schools today. High stakes testings means using test results to make important policy decisions, such as student promotion or retention and special class placement. Given the uses and social consequences of tests, some suggest that the social consequences of testing and measurement should be considered in specifications of validity (e.g., Cronbach, 1980; Messick, 1975). In other words, validity should be concerned not only with the technical dimensions discussed in this chapter but also with the consequences of a specific form of measurement. For example, if we are using behavioral observations to determine children's social competence, we should be concerned with the traditionally framed issues of construct, content, predictive, and concurrent validity. Assuming that these validity concerns are all met, we still must be concerned with ethical and social consequences if this instrument is to be used in a school system as one of many measures to determine whether children will be promoted from or retained in kindergarten. Validity is tricky stuff, and we should remain humble and open as we address it.

THINGS TO THINK ABOUT

1. We know that observer bias is a problem in observational research. Ways to alleviate this problem often involve having access to more than one observer. How could observer bias be minimized in situations where only one observer is used?

_____

_____

_____

_____

_____

_____

2. How does your knowledge of reliability and validity affect the ways in which you construct behavioral categories?

_____

_____

_____

_____

_____

_____

2a. As an exercise, choose a construct (such as aggression or intelligence) and complete a matrix of sample–sign and molecular–molar dimensions for those constructs.

_____

_____

_____

_____

_____

_____

_____

_____

2b. How would you go about determining different forms of validity for each of the measures?

_____

_____

_____

_____

_____

_____

GLOSSARY

Homogeneity: The degree to which the elements within composite measures are all interrelated; measured by split-half reliability.

Give your example:

_____

_____

_____

_____

Kappa: A measure of observer reliability that corrects for chance agree and is expressed from −1.0 to +1.0.

Molar: A measure that is an aggregate of molecular measures. For example, aggression has a number of molecular components.
 Give your example:

_____

_____

_____

_____

_____

Molecular: A measure that is expressed behaviorally in terms of minute behaviors. For example, bite, punch, and scratch are molecular behaviors that relate to the molar category aggression.
 Give your example:

_____

_____

_____

_____

_____

Observer Drift: Changes in observers' scoring of the same behaviors across time.
 Give your example:

_____

_____

_____

_____

Observer fatigue: When observer boredom or fatigue results in inaccurate scoring.
Give your example:

_____

_____

_____

_____

_____

Occurrence/Nonoccurrence: A measure of observer reliability expressed as a percentage but with the possibility of chance agreements omitted.

Percentage of agreement: A measure of observer reliability, expressed as the percentage of observers agreeing.

Reactivity: A situation in which participants being observed act unnaturally in reaction to being observed.
Give your example:

_____

_____

_____

_____

_____

Reliability: Consistency of observations across time and observers.

Reliability, interobserver: The degree to which multiple observers agree on what they see.

Reliability, intraobserver: The degree to which one observer scores consistently across time.

Reliability, split-half: The degree to which odd and even measures are consistent, or homogeneous.

Reliability, test-retest: Consistency in measures across time.

Resolution: Changes in behavior reflected in changes in scoring.
Give your example:

_____

_____

_____

_____

_____

Sample/Sign: Measure of behavior that indexes a level of abstraction where sample is an actual behavior, such as punch, and sign is an abstraction that is not directly observable, such as aggression.
Give your example:

_____

_____

_____

_____

_____

Sensitivity: The extent to which changes in behavior are reflected in measured values.
Give your example:

_____

_____

_____

_____

_____

Smaller/Larger index: A measure of interobserver reliability in which two measures of the same behavior, the smaller and the larger, are compared.

Stability: Similarity in measurement across time, as measured by test–retest reliability.
Give your example:

_____

_____

_____

_____

_____

Validity: Truthfulness.
Give your example:

_____

_____

_____

_____

_____

Validity, construct: The truthfulness of a nonobservable, theoretical entity, such as aggression.
Give your example:

_____

_____

_____

_____

_____

Validity, content: A case in which the instrument used in measurement represents what it purports to measure.

Give your example:

_____

_____

_____

_____

_____

_____

Validity, criterion: Composed of predictive validity (i.e., where a behavior accurately predicts something) and concurrent validity (i.e., where a behavior is related to a similar measure, taken contemporaneously).

Give your example:

_____

_____

_____

_____

_____

_____

8

Units Of Analysis

In this chapter, I discuss the ways in which we organize our categories and measures of behavior so that they can be counted. Recall in earlier chapters the discussion of the ways in which categories were formed (Chapter 5) and the ways in which those categories could be measured (Chapter 6). In this chapter, consideration is given to the next step: how we group individual measures of behavior so that they can be counted and analyzed statistically.

To this end, I discuss the ways in which these categories can be counted. Specifically, I discuss independence of units of analysis. Units of analysis refer to the units that will be subjected to statistical testing. For example, in studying children in a classroom we may have the category of student question. The unit of analysis becomes the way in which we count occurrences of this category: Do we use the individual child or the classroom as the unit of analysis? Such choices have important implications for the meaning of our data.

INDEPENDENCE OF MEASUREMENT

The notion of independence of behavioral measures is an important one. By independence I mean, generally, that people or behaviors being observed are assumed to be unrelated to each other. This assumed independence is particularly important for people utilizing parametric statistical procedures. These statistical procedures assume that individual observations and individual participants have been sampled randomly and thus are independent; any relations among the variables should be the hypothesized relations. The implications of violating independence assumptions are that within-group error variance is minimized and, correspondingly, the probability of rejecting the null hypothesis is increased (see Applebaum & McCall, 1983, for a more detailed description of the statistical implications). The null hypothesis assumes no between-group differences and no associations among measures. The null is rejected when differences or associations are found.

In everyday language, violating independence assumptions typically results in maximizing between-group differences and inflating statistical significance. In this section, I outline some of the more commonly occurring threats to independence as well as some ways avoid them. These threats and possible solutions, in the order in which they are discussed, are displayed in Fig. 8.1.

Pooling

Pooling fallacy is a term introduced by Machlis (cited in Martin & Bateson, 1993). Pooling occurs when separate observations, not individual participants, are treated as the unit of analysis. For example we may have observed 25 third graders ($N = 25$) 10 times during their recess period, for a total of 250 observations. The pooling fallacy is treating the N as 250, not as 25. In this case we want to generalize our results to children not to observations; therefore, N should be 25 participants, not 250. The separate observations of each child are not independent of each other and should not be treated as such. Specifically, each individual's behavior should be related from observation 1 though 10; individual children should be different from each other, and children should be treated as the unit of measurement. To treat individual observations not as separate units violates the independence assumption.

A recent report by Leger and Didrichson (1994), however, suggested that individual observations can be used as the unit of analysis when intraindividual variance exceeds interindividual variance. That is, scores from separate observations can be used when the variability of individuals' behavior from one observation to the next is greater than the variation between individuals. Simply, the individuals' observations are not interdependent.

Contiguous Behaviors

A related issue involves contiguous observations of individuals: Should we treat these individual scores as separate scores or aggregate the multiple observations on each participant for specific sessions? In the example of recess observations,

Threats	Possible Solutions
Pooling	N = Subjects, not observations
Contiguous observations	Aggregate within session
Interrelated categories	Keep mutually exclusive
	Recognize subscore dependence
Litter/group effects	Group, not individual, as unit deviation scores
	Individual and group factors

FIG. 8.1.   Some threats and solutions to non-independence of observation scores.

suppose that each individual child in the class were observed every 2 minutes for a 20-minute recess period; thus, each child is observed 10 times per recess period. The issue here relates to the way in which we treat the individual observations of each child. Do we treat each of the 10 observations within one period as a separate score for that child or do we aggregate all 10 scores into one observation? Certainly, the latter approach is more conservative to the extent that children's behaviors across a 20-minute recess period are probably interrelated. For example, if we have children playing football at time 1, they probably will be playing football at time 10; thus, each recess period would yield one observation per child. Treating separate observations within the recess period as distinct measurement points assumes that each is independent. In this case, they probably are not independent.

It becomes an interesting empirical problem, however, to determine what time lag between observations is necessary before we can treat separate, contiguous observations of individuals as independent. Time is clearly an issue, but it is unclear what time span is enough. Certainly, the nature of the task is relevant here. We may be able to treat free behaviors as one set of observations and teacher-led games during the same period as another set of observations. As a rule of thumb, we might consider aggregating individuals' contiguous behavior within theoretically or empirically distinct behavioral categories or events.

Interrelated Categories

Determining the extent to which behavioral categories are independent is another issue. As discussed in Chapter 5, observational categories should be homogeneous (i.e., composed of interrelated components) and mutually exclusive (i.e., they must not be different ways of measuring the same construct). Of course, two distinct categories (such as physical attractiveness and peer popularity) can be interdependent for reasons other than redundancy. Here, we are concerned with behavioral categories that are interdependent because of behavioral overlap. For example, a category labeled *smile* shares similar behavioral attributes with a category labeled *positive affect*. Thus, these two categories should probably be aggregated into a molar category called *positive affect display*.

Categories can also be interdependent because of the ways in which we measure them. For example, in my (Pellegrini, 1993) research on children's rough-and-tumble play (R&T), I measured the relative frequency with which children engage in R&T (i.e., the proportion of outdoor behavior that is R&T) as well as the variety of the behaviors comprising R&T (i.e., the number of different R&T behaviors exhibited by a participant). These two measures, obviously, are interdependent in that the variety measure is derived from the proportion measure. We may want to consider these measures as separate for theoretical reasons, but we should not lose sight of their statistical interdependence.

Litter or Group Effects

The last independence issue, labeled *litter effects* by Martin and Bateson (1993), is probably the most commonly violated. Litter effects refer directly to the interdependence of behavior of litter mates, such as siblings; they can also refer to the interdependence of nonkin individuals who are part of the same social grouping. For example, it is common in one branch of educational research, product-process research, to observe quartets of students interacting around a task. Typically in this research tradition, individuals' utterances and behaviors (called processes) are coded and then related to some dimension of task performance (i.e., the product). Furthermore, if there are 10 groups of 4, the N is typically considered as 40, not 10. Thus, individuals within each group are treated as if they are independent of the other individuals in that group. This seems problematic: To say that the behavior of individual children in quartets is independent of the others is like saying that the following two utterances by two members of a groups are independent of each other.

Speaker 1: What time is it?

Speaker 2: 3:30.

Obviously, when people interact with each other as part of a group, individual behaviors are related to the behaviors of the group members. Thus, in the preceding example, the quartet, not the individual, should be treated as the unit of analysis. Similar problems of interdependence are faced when conducting observations in classrooms. Individual children's social behaviors within one classroom are probably interrelated to the extent that each child has an effect on other children. Additionally, each child is influenced by the classroom teacher. In this case, the classroom may be the appropriate unit of analysis.

ADDRESSING THE PROBLEMS OF INTERDEPENDENCE

Obviously these issues put the observer or researcher against some logistical problems, such as having to observe a larger number of classrooms rather than observing individuals within fewer classrooms. This problem may be resolved by working with a research design utilizing smaller samples, such as classrooms rather than children within classrooms. If independence assumptions are violated, one can choose a larger sample, say 25 children from each of two classes for an N of 50 rather than 2. Alternatively, the two classrooms could be treated as replication samples. In this case results would be accepted if they replicated in both groups.

There are situations, however, in which we are interested in the ways individuals within groups interact; it is then important to untangle group and individual effects. For example, if we have a boy and a girl playing, on separate occasions, with male-preferred and female-preferred toys, we might want to know the way in which each child interacts with the specific toys. This would not be possible if we were to treat the dyad as the unit of analysis. A number of solutions have been proffered to address this issue, and two are discussed here: investigating deviation scores and treating individuals within groups as separate factors in data analyses.

Deviation scores involve individual scores for a specific behavior minus the group score for that same behavior. Following the boy–girl dyad example, Jane Perlmutter and I (Pellegrini & Perlmutter, 1989) studied same- and mixed-gender dyads of preschool children playing with different toys. We coded their play along nine dimensions (such as interactive-dramatic and solitary-constructive) and their utterances along six dimensions (such as commands and imitations). For same-gender dyads, dyads were the unit of analysis; that is, scores from both individuals within the dyad were aggregated to yield a male score for male dyads and a female score for the female dyads. For mixed-gender dyads, deviation scores were calculated for each dyad such that an individual's score for commands, for example, would equal his or her individual score minus the commands for that dyad. In this way the individual's behavior is considered as a dimension of the group processes. Others, such as Cronbach (1976), has discussed variations of the deviation score method.

Additionally, separate individual scores can be treated as individual factors. This procedure is relevant to those researchers using factorial designs and analyses of variance in their data analyses. Because this is not a statistics book, I touch on this only briefly, and the interested reader is referred to Applebaum and McCall (1983) for a full and very understandable treatment of data analysis techniques. In the play example, we have three factors in our analyses, gender of target (2: boys and girls), gender of partner (2: boys and girls), and the type of toy. In this way we can examine the extent to which boys with girl partners give commands while playing with male-preferred toys.

It is important to consider the interdependence of participants in social interaction. Observers, however, cannot assume that all social groupings result in interdependent social behavior; thus, some preanalyses, both theoretical and empirical, are necessary. As discussed by Applebaum and McCall (1983), the exam scores of a group of undergraduates in a class should not be treated as interdependent scores. On the other hand, their discussions in the classroom, after and before the exam, are almost certain to be interdependent. In short, much but not all of group behavior is interdependent. Where this is the case, care needs to be taken so that the individual and group contributions are untangled.

SUMMARY AND CONCLUSIONS

In this chapter, I have addressed some particular problems associated with organizing measures of behavior so that they can be counted. Information presented in this chapter extends the information that was presented in earlier chapters on categories and measures of behavior. The information from this chapter is crucial as we consider statistical analyses of our data (to be discussed in Chapter 9). Again, planning is necessary to determine the appropriate unit of analysis. If we ignore preplanning, the quality of the data suffer. When we violate independence assumptions we skew our results toward accepting our hypothesis and rejecting the null hypothesis. The unit of analysis that we choose should clearly relate to the questions we have in mind.

THINGS TO THINK ABOUT

1. Describe two classroom scenarios in which the classroom should be the unit of analysis and two in which individuals within those classrooms should be the unit.

_____

_____

_____

_____

_____

_____

GLOSSARY

Contiguous observations: Observation points that are next to each other, for example, observations conducted on the same child every 2 minutes.

Give your example:

_____

_____

_____

_____

_____

Deviation score: An individual score expressed in terms of its deviation from the score of the group in which the individual is embedded. For example, a child's score for words spoken is expressed as his or her words minus the average number of words spoken by the group in which the target child is embedded.

Give your example:

_____

_____

Litter effects: Situations in which members of a group influence the score of an individual. For example, one child's social interaction score could be influenced by the social interaction of his or her peers.

Give your example:

Pooling: In this chapter pooling refers to the use of individual observations as the unit of analysis. For example if we have 10 children observed 20 times, the N, or number of subjects, is 10, not 200 (i.e., the number of observations for each child).

Give your example:

Population/universe: The group of people or behaviors from which we sample. A population of people could be all the children in a particular school or state; the universe of behaviors could be all the behaviors that children exhibit.

Give your example:

_____

_____

_____

Sample: A representation of the whole population or universe. For example, a sample of children may represent the population of a city of state. Similarly, a sample of play behaviors may represent the universe of children's behavioral acts.

Give your example:

_____

_____

_____

_____

_____

9

Elementary Statistics for Use With Observational Data

In this chapter, I outline procedures for calculating some basic statistics. The aim of the chapter is not to provide an exhaustive discussion of statistics and statistical procedures. My intent in this chapter is to present a sampler of statistical terms and procedures to organize, analyze, and interpret observational data. To this end, I outline basic descriptive statistics, then inferential statistics.

DESCRIPTIVE STATISTICS

Descriptive statistics should be the first level of organizing observational data. In this section, I discuss measures of central tendency (mean, median, and mode) as well as measures of variability (range, variance, and standard deviation). These measures are summarized and displayed in Fig. 9.1.

Measures of central tendency are indicative of some typical score from a sample. When considering measures of central tendency and all other statistical measures, one should keep in mind the unit of analysis issues, as discussed in Chapter 8. For example, are we describing individual children in a group, or are we describing the group? Thus, review of that chapter may be useful before proceeding with data analyses.

Probably the most common measure of central tendency is the *mean*, or average. The mean can be represented as $\overline{X}$ or M. M is calculated by summing all the values and then dividing that sum by the number of values. For example, let us say that we have the activity ratings (each of which varies from 1 to 9) for 10 children during one recess period. The numbers for this are displayed in Table 9.1. The sum, or Σ, of all values, 60, is divided by the number of values (N):

$$\frac{60}{10} = 6$$

Central Tendency	Variability
Mean	Range
Median	Variance
Mode	Standard deviation

FIG. 9.1.   Measures of central tendency and variability.

TABLE 9.1
Example for Central Tendencies and Variability Measures

Child	Rating	$(xi - \overline{X})$	$(xi - \overline{X})^2$
1	4	−2	4
2	5	−1	1
3	4	−2	4
4	6	0	0
5	9	3	9
6	6	0	0
7	7	1	1
8	8	2	4
9	2	−4	16
10	9	3	9
N = 10	Σ = 60		$\Sigma(xi - \overline{x})^2 = 48$
			$s^2 = 48/9 = 5.3$
			$s = 2.30$

The median is another measure of central tendency. The *median* is simply the middle score in the list of scores, arranged from highest to lowest. It is sometimes used instead of the mean when samples are small and when a few extreme scores unduly influence the mean score. In the case of the data displayed in Table 9.1, we have an even number of scores, so we take the average of the two middle scores. The scores from this figure can be ordered as 2, 4, 4, 5, 6, 6, 7, 8, 9, 9. In this case the median is the average of the 6 and 6; thus, 6 is the median. In the case the median is identical to the mean value for the same scores.

The *mode* score represents the most frequently occurring score. In this case we have a multimodal distribution because there are three modes: 4, 6, and 9. Like median scores, modes can be used with small samples, especially when the samples are characterized by extreme, "outlier" scores.

Scores can be represented by some typical central tendency score and the extent to which a set of scores varies around that central score. At the simplest level, the range indicates the difference between the highest score and the lowest score. For the values presented in Table 9.1, the largest score is 9 and the lowest is 2; thus the range = 9 – 2 = 7.

Variance (s^2) and its square root, *standard deviation* (*s* or *SD*), are more common measures of variability. Both s^2 and *SD* are measures of the degree to which scores vary from the mean. To calculate s^2, we take each score, or xi, and subtract from it the mean of the scores, or $\_$ of which the individual score is a part. Next, we square each of these differences, X add them together, and divide by the total minus 1, or $N - 1$. This whole procedure is illustrated in Table 9.1. As can be seen from the calculations illustrated on the right side of the table, s^2 equals 5.3; *s*, or the square root of s^2 equals 2.30. *s* indicates that for these distribution of scores, the mean is 10, but the typical score varies around that mean by 2.30, so the typical score is 10 ± 2.30. Thus, the mean and the standard deviations, taken together, are excellent indicators of typical scores in a distributions. The standard formula for s^2 follows:

$$s^2 = \frac{\Sigma(xi - \bar{x})}{N - 1}$$

INFERENTIAL STATISTICS

Parametric and Nonparametric Statistics

Descriptive statistics are useful to illustrate the nature of the data collected. In this section, I discuss inferential statistics. Inferential statistics enable us to use the data we have collected from our sample to make inferences about a larger group (McCall, 1980). Inferential statistics also allow us to determine the extent to which the results we have obtained are due to chance.

I briefly discuss two families of statistical techniques: parametric and nonparametric statistics. A *parameter*, in statistical terms, is a characteristic of a population (McCall, 1980). Thus, with parametric statistics we test a sample and make judgments, or inferences, about a larger population of which our sample is representative. Populations are represented in a normal distribution. On the other hand, with nonparametric statistics, we do not make judgments about a population; thus, nonparametric statistics are sometimes referred to as distribution free. We do, however, make inferences about the probability of specific occurrences within a sample being due to chance. For our purposes the relevant difference between these two families of statistical procedures relates to application.

Generally, parametric statistics, because they make judgments about a population, are more restrictive than nonparametric statistics. These restrictions apply to the nature of the sample from which we collect data and are displayed in Table 9.2.

Nonparametric tests are necessary when certain scales of measurement are used, specifically nominal and ordinal scales. In the first case, if we are interested in the relation between gender (i.e., a nominal scale) and children's behavior on different types of playgrounds (i.e., also a nominal scale), then a nonparametric procedure is warranted. Regarding ordinal data, nonparametrics would be useful if we were

TABLE 9.2
Restrictions for Parametric Statistics

	Parametric	*Nonparametric*
Scale	Interval ratio	Nominal, ordinal
Distribution	Normal	Normal or skewed

interested in the relation between children's dominance status (i.e., an ordinal measure) and sociometric status (i.e., a nominal scale). Interval and ratio data can be used in parametric procedures.

Nonparametric statistics are often preferred when the variables that we measure from our samples are not normally distributed. It is often the case that small samples do not meet normality assumptions. However, statistics can be used when normality assumptions are violated, particularly if we have a large sample (McCall, 1980). It should be noted that the degree to which assumptions of statistical procedures are violated diminishes their value.

In the remainder of this chapter, I outline some statistical procedures, both parametric and nonparametric, for use with observational data. The interested reader is referred to a number of different sources for an extended discussion. Siegel (1956) wrote the classic nonparametric book almost 40 years ago, but it is still very useful. Discussion of related issues can also be found in Hollander and Wolfe (1973), Kerlinger (1973), and McCall (1980).

Basic Inferential Statistics

Inferential statistics help us determine the degree to which our results differ from chance occurrence. The gauging of chance level can be quantified in terms of probability. Thus, we can say that the scores from two groups are different at a specific probability level. Similarly, we can attach a probability statement to the relation between two variables, like the relation between physical attractiveness and popularity. The probability value tells us the extent to which the observed difference or relation is due to chance. Traditionally, researchers have used a probability level, or p level, of .05 to indicate statistical significance (see Cohen, 1994, for a recent critique of the .05 criterion). In the remainder of this chapter, I outline some basic inferential statistics that address differences and associations.

Statistics for Detecting Differences. These statistical procedures can be applied to determining differences between and within groups. For example, to what degree are children in three different experimental classrooms different in terms of language skills? In short, the statistical procedures outlined in this section help determine the extent to which a set or sets of things is greater than other sets.

Differences can be measured within and across individuals or groups, as discussed in Chapter 8. For example, what are the language differences in a group of children as they develop across the first 3 years? When comparing the same children's language at year 1 and at year 3 we are examining differences between

TABLE 9.3
Parametric and Nonparametric Statistics for Detecting Differences

	Correlated groups	Uncorrelated groups
Parametric	t test	t test
	Repeated-measures ANOVA	ANOVA
Nonparametric	Fisher sign	Mann–Whitney
	Wilcoxon sign rank	Kruskal–Wallis

related or *correlated groups*. Specifically, the group at year 1 and the group at year 3 are the same group, though they differ in terms of age; these individuals are related in a statistical sense. An example of uncorrelated groups would be two different groups of children, one group at year 1 and another at year 3. A variety of procedures for measuring between group differences for both correlated and uncorrelated groups is displayed in Table 9.3. I do not derive most of the formulas as there are numerous statistics texts that can accomplish that task much better than I. Furthermore, most personal and laptop computers have programs, like SPSS (Norusis, 1988a, 1988b), to compute these statistics. I merely explicate when each of a variety of techniques can be used.

Beginning with parametric statistics the basic statistic for comparing two groups is the *t* test, and it can be used for both correlated and independent (i.e., uncorrelated) groups. We could use a *t* test to determine the difference in play behaviors when the same group of children (i.e., correlated groups) played with two separate sets of toys. The *t* test would tell us the degree to which the difference in play in each setting was beyond chance. An example using uncorrelated groups is the comparison of the play behaviors of two different groups of children, each of whom plays with one set of toys.

The analysis of variance (ANOVA) is like the *t* test but it is used when more than two groups are being compared. For example, three age groups of children may be playing with a set of toys. We would code their play behaviors and then compare the means among the three groups with ANOVA techniques. If the same children are playing with three sets of toys, we can compare the means in each of the three settings with a repeated-measures ANOVA. ANOVAs can include more than one factor. The one-way ANOVA used in this example could be expanded to include gender at two levels and age at three levels.

Next, we move into the nonparametric world. Perhaps the simplest of all techniques to compare two groups is Fisher's sign test. With this test for correlated samples we simply score a + or − every time a difference in a particular direction is observed for each subject. Then we compare the number of +s with the number of subjects observed and look up that value in a binomial distribution table. Table 9.4 shows data for illustration.

In this case, we have 10 children whose aggression was observed while they played with two sets of toys on separate occasions. We coded the number of aggressive acts for each child with each set of toys. We hypothesized that toy set 1 would elicit more aggression than set 2. Thus, for each child, when a larger value

TABLE 9.4
Data Used in Fisher's Sign Test

Subject	Aggression With Toy 1	Aggression With Toy 2	Toy 1 > Toy 2
1	5	3	+
2	3	1	+
3	1	0	+
4	7	2	+
5	3	5	−
6	10	6	+
7	5	4	+
8	2	0	+
9	4	1	+
10	6	5	+

Note. S + = 9:10; $p < .01$.

was observed in set 1 than in set 2, a + was tallied. We see that in 9 of 10 cases more aggression was observed with set 1 than with set 2; when this ratio is indexed in a binomial table, it is beyond chance. In other words, when children play with toys in set 1 they are more aggressive, at a probability of .01, than when they play with toys in set 2.

The simplicity of the sign test should not put you off. Actually, simplicity is a virtue. If a procedure tells you what you need, you should use it. If you are simply interested in the answer to yes/no or greater than/less than questions, without concern for the magnitude of the difference, then the sign test may be for you.

The disadvantages to this procedure are that it does not consider the magnitude of differences between groups and that it is a statistically conservative procedure. That is, compared to other tests of differences, it is relatively difficult to reject the null hypothesis (thus maximizing the possibility of Type II error).

Another nonparametric test that can be used with correlated groups and takes into account the magnitude of differences is the Wilcoxon sign rank test. With this procedure, individuals within each condition, say within toy set 1 and within toy set 2, are rank ordered from largest to smallest. Thus, the magnitude of differences is considered.

Moving to the independent group nonparametric tests we have the Mann–Whitney U test and the Kruskal–Wallis test. The Mann–Whitney test is a nonparametric equivalent to the t test; it is used to detect differences between two groups. The Kruskal–Wallis test is the nonparametric equivalent to the ANOVA and is useful in detecting between-group differences when more than two groups are involved. The derivations of each of these formulae are available in a number of basic statistics books (e.g., McCall, 1980) and are available in package form for use on personal computers (SPSS; Norusis, 1988a).

To summarize, in this section I addressed the extent to which data for specified groups were different from each other. These statistical procedures are often used in service of making causal arguments. Take, for example, the example presented previously of comparing the effects of two toy sets. Children in this hypothetical experiment were exposed to two sets of toys and their aggression was measured while they played with each. That more aggression was observed with set 1 than with set 2 allowed us to infer that the toys in set 1 caused the aggression. Suffice it to say that causality can be inferred only from experimental data (see Pellegrini, 1991, for a discussion of causality and experiments) or through the use of causal models and structural equations (see the special issue of *Child Development*, 1987) for a review of various procedures).

Statistics to Measure Associations.   In this section, I discuss associations. By association I mean that two sets of variables co-occur in systematic ways. Correlation coefficients are measures of association. Association between two variables, as has been drilled into most of our heads like a catechism, does not allow us to make causal inferences. The variables are related to the extent that they tend to co-occur; that is, there is a correlation between a set of variables. For example, there may be a correlation between two sets of variables, like popularity and prosocial behavior, but it does not mean that one causes the other. Caution when discussing correlations is for some of us obligatory and routinized. Now that I have performed my duties, I go on to discuss correlations.

Correlation coefficients are useful in a number of ways to observational researchers. As I noted in the discussion of reliability and validity (Chapter 7), they can be used to gauge interobserver reliability as well as concurrent and predictive validity. Correlation coefficients vary from -1.0 to $+1.0$. The magnitude of the correlation refers to the level of correspondence between the two variables. If there is a 1:1 correspondence, there will be a perfect correlation. For example, if we had a measure of popularity (x) that varied from 1 to 5 and a measure of prosocial behavior (y) that varied from 1 to 10, a perfect correlation would mean that each variation in x corresponds to an exact variation in y. A correlation of $+1.0$ would indicate a 1:1 correspondence between measures of popularity and prosocial behavior for a child; the more prosocial the behavior, the more popular the child. A negative correlation would indicate that the more popular a child, the less prosocial behavior he or she would exhibit. A 0 correlation means the two variables are independent of each other; that is, there is no relation between them.

Of course, we rarely observe perfect correlations; most are somewhere in between. Correlation coefficients (r), like other inferential statistics, have probability levels attached to them. Statistical significance, as I have noted already, depends on the level of the statistic, in this case the magnitude of the correlation coefficient, and the number of subjects (N). An r of .49 is statistically significant, $p < .05$, when $N = 12$ but not when $N = 11$! Probability statements tell us the likelihood that the correlation coefficient is due to chance. A significant r simply tells you that a systematic relation between two variables exits. It does not tell you about its size or importance (Martin & Bateson, 1993).

We can assign meaning to a correlation coefficient, however, by squaring it: If r = .49, then R^2 = .24. The R^2 statistic is meaningful in that it tells us the degree to which the variation in x explains variation in y. Regarding the popularity example, we can say that popularity explains 24% of the variation in prosocial behavior. The R^2 approach to interpreting the meaning of a correlation coefficient is intuitively useful in that it gives us an idea of how much we can explain in a relation. Knowing that an r is statistically significant is useful, initially, in that it tells us that the association is not due to chance. The R^2 adds more information by explaining the amount of variation explained. It could be the case, for example that we have a statistically significant correlation coefficient, say of .2, but the R^2 would indicate that the variable only explains 4% of the variation; thus, 96% of the variation remains unexplained.

There are parametric and nonparametric correlation coefficients. The Pearson product–moment correlation coefficient is the parametric coefficient and is represented by r. It is a measure of the linear relation between two variables. The Pearson r is a statistical representation of the extent to which a scatterplot of the points for two variables fall on a line. In the case of a perfect correlation, the points fall along a line. In less than perfect correlations, the points cluster to various degrees around, not on, a line.

The nonparametric correlation coefficients, Spearman's rank-order correlation represented by rs, and Kendall's tau, represented by t, measure associations, but the associations do not necessarily have to be linear, as they must with r. The equivalence between r and rs is close, but the latter typically yields a lower value (Guilford & Fruchter, 1973; McCall, 1980). Thus, they can be interpreted similarly in terms of probability. The rs is probably more useful with smaller samples, and Kendall's tau is useful with intermediate samples (McCall, 1980).

Another very common technique for measuring the association between sets of variables, particularly nominal measures, is the chi-square, represented as c2. Chi-square is useful if we want to determine the independence of two sets of measures, say child-oriented classrooms and teacher satisfaction with child's school experience. Most basically, we could divide each of the two groups into high and low, yielding high and low orientation and high and low groups. Chi-square analyses are best understood when displayed in matrix form, as in Fig. 9.2 (Kerlinger, 1973). The frequencies in the matrix represent the distribution of different levels of parental satisfaction with each form of classroom. We want to know if a systematic relation exists between classroom orientation and parental satisfaction.

	Child-oriented/High	Child-oriented/Low	Total
Teacher Sat/High	47	35	82
Teacher Sat/Low	5	21	26
Total	52	56	108

FIG. 9.2.   Chi-square matrix.

To determine the association we subject the data in the matrix to the equation

$$\chi^2 = \frac{[fo - fe]^2}{[fe]}$$

$$\chi^2 = \frac{(60 - 50)^2}{50} + \frac{(40 - 50)^2}{50} = \frac{100}{50} + \frac{100}{50} = 4$$

The chi-square value is 4. To determine the statistical significance of the value we identify the degrees of freedom (1) and look up the value in a chi-square table to find that it corresponds to $p < .05$.

In short, chi-square analysis is a quick and easy method for determining the association between sets of measures.

Sequences of Behavior.   Like the other statistical procedures reviewed thus far, different types of sequential analyses have been outlined and discussed in a number of different places. The interested reader is referred to Bakeman and Gottman (1986) for a thorough introduction and to Bakeman and Quera (in prep) and Gottman and Roy (1990) for more advanced discussions. In this section, I discuss briefly the uses of sequential analyses and calculate a simple example.

As the name states, sequential analysis is concerned with the way in which behaviors unfold in order. We can be concerned with the order of the events (i.e., event sequences), for example $1 \rightarrow 2 \rightarrow 3$. Additionally, we can be concerned with the temporal dimension associated with the order (i.e., time sequences; Bakeman & Gottman, 1986), for example, 1 (duration: 20 seconds) $\rightarrow$ 2 (duration 45 seconds). Even at the simpler level, sequential analyses allow the observer and then the reader to get an accurate picture of the ways in which behaviors unfold in time. After all, behaviors are embedded in a larger behavioral stream. If we want to describe a behavior accurately, we should also describe the ways in which it unfolds. Additionally, sequential information helps us to understand the meaning of a behavior. That is, we can make inferences about the meaning of behavior A by what follows it. For example, we can make inferences about the meaning of R&T if it is followed by aggression with a high degree of consistency.

The degree to which events follow each other can be expressed in terms of probabilities (Bakeman & Gottman, 1986). An unconditional probability is just a relative frequency score. For example, if we are interested in R&T and games, unconditional probabilities are the ratios of each measure to the total scores. For example, if we observed a total of 500 separate events, 15 of which were R&T and 5 of which were games, the unconditional probabilities of R&T and games would be .03 and .01, respectively.

A conditional probability is more fine-tuned; it indicates the probability of a behavior of interest, say games, in relation to another term, say R&T. Again, it's simply a case of dividing the behavior of interest, games, by R&T: 5/15 = .33.

A transitional probability indicates the probability that one behavior is followed by another behavior. Continuing with the example, the transitional probability informs us of the probability of R&T $\rightarrow$ games.

To test transitional probabilities we construct transitional models. For example, we might have a 2-state model of R&T leading to aggression and another 2-state model of R&T leading to games. Constructing separate 2-state models, rather than 3-, 4-, and 5-state models, is most sensible in social and behavioral science because of the large sample demands of the more involved models (Bakeman & Gottman, 1986).

In the example to follow I list a hypothetical occurrence of behavioral events wherein we have three mutually exclusive codes: R&T (A), games (B), and other (C). We coded the following stream of events:

ABBABAACABABACBCCAAB

From this stream we constructed a transitional frequency matrix, as displayed in Fig. 9.3 (Bakeman & Gottman, 1986).

Figure 9.4 displays the sequence of each of the pairs of behaviors, derived from the stream presented previously. A is followed by A, 0 and A is followed by B, 4, and so on. The 6 in the margin of the A row indicates the frequency of sequences in which A was observed at lag 0. Lag 0 is the point of origin of sequential analysis; for example, if we examine the relation between R&T and aggression, R&T is at Lag 0 and aggression is at Lag 1. The next step is to construct, from these numbers, a transitional probability matrix. This matrix, displayed in Fig. 9.5 indicates the transitional probability of various 2-state transitions. The individual transitional probabilities are derived by dividing the value in the cell of interest by the value at the end of the corresponding row. The information in this figure suggests that the probability of R&T (A) moving to games (B) is .66; similarly, the probability of games moving to R&T is .66.

The next, question is to what degree do these probability statements occur by chance. In other words, can we attach statistical significance, or p value, to these probability levels. The answer is yes. The reader is referred to Bakeman and Gottman (1986) for the procedures necessary to derive expected frequencies for matrices and then convert the value to z scores.

A simpler procedure is to use the Fisher's Sign Test, discussed earlier in this chapter, to test a specific hypothesis, say that R&T leads to games at a significant rate. Using the data from Fig. 9.4, we test the significance of A → B. The frequency of A → B was 4 out of 6 observations in which A was observed at lag 0. We look up the probability of 4 of 6 positive signs and see it is statistically significant.

		Lag 1			
		A	*B*	*C*	
	A	0	4	2	6
Lag 0	*B*	2	0	1	3
	C	1	0	0	1
					10

FIG. 9.3. Transitional frequency matrix.

		Lag 1		
		A	B	C
Lag 0	A	0	.66	.33
	B	.66	0	.33
	C	1.00	0	0

FIG. 9.4   Transitional probability matrix.

Before finishing with sequential analyses I briefly note an interobserver reliability problem that is unique to sequential analyses (Hollenbeck, 1978; Sackett, 1978). Sequential analyses can be event-based or time-based. Reliability applied to both strategies involves matching two observers' codings of similar events. Consequently, the two observers' coding of the sequences must match, or the sequences will not be aligned (Hollenbeck, 1978): Observer 1 could be coding the one AB series, and observer 2 could be coding a different AB series. Misalignment is typically caused by just one disagreement. One way to minimize this problem is to make sure that all observers are beginning at exactly the same time. Then, set a time limit for coding the next sequence. If disagreement occurs during that time score it as a disagreement, then begin again, simultaneously observing at the same point, repeating the process. In short, observers must be sure they are scoring the same sequences at the same time.

SUMMARY AND CONCLUSIONS

In this chapter, I have reviewed some very elementary statistical procedures that can be used with observational data. As stated at the beginning and throughout the chapter, my intent is not to be exhaustive and authoritative. I merely wanted to expose the reader to some of the techniques available that can help to describe data and to make inferences about them. The citations made throughout this chapter provide useful guides.

Most encouraging is the availability of various statistical packages, such as SPSS, on personal computers. People can go to most university bookstores, purchase this software, and load it onto their own computers. The availability of software varies from very simple (i.e., only descriptive statistics are presented) to more complex models. Additionally, with the advent of laptop and notebook computers and mechanical data recording devices (discussed in Chapter 10), statistical packages can be built in to the machines we use to collect the observational data. In short, the extant technology makes statistical analysis of observational data very easy indeed. Statistical sophistication, however, is never a substitute for an interesting question.

GLOSSARY

Analysis of Variance (ANOVA): A parametric statistical that tests for differences among three or more groups.
  Give your example:

_____

_____

_____

_____

Associations: Whether or not two measures are related. For example, smoking and lung disease are associated.
  Give your example:

_____

_____

_____

_____

Central tendency scores: A typical score. Mean, median, and mode are examples.

Correlation coefficient: Expressed as r, it is a measurement of the association between two variables.
  Give your example:

_____

_____

_____

_____

Inferential Statistics: Statistical techniques that make inferences about the extent to which computed values differ from chance. Some techniques make inferences about a population.

Kruskal–Wallis Test: The nonparametric equivalent to the ANOVA.

Mann–Whitney Test: The nonparametric equivalent to the t test.

Median: The score in the middle of a distribution.

Mean: The average score of a distribution.

Mode: The most frequently occurring score(s) in a distribution.

Nonparametric statistics: Inferential statistical techniques that do not make inferences to a population.

Parametric statistics: Inferential statistical techniques that make inferences about a population.

Probability: The likelihood that a finding is due to chance, expressed as p.

Probability, conditional: In sequential analysis, this refers to the relative frequency of one behavior in relation to another specific behavior.

Probability, transitional: In sequential analyses, this is the probability that one behavior is followed by another.

Probability, unconditional: In sequential analyses, one behavior is expressed in terms of its relative frequency to all other behaviors.

Range: The degree to which a set of scores varies from the high to the low points.

Sequential analysis: A statistical technique for determining the association between sequences of behaviors.

Sign Test: A nonparametric test that measures differences without concern for the degree of difference.

Standard deviation: The deviation scores (from the mean) in a set.

Statistical significance: Traditionally expressed as $p < .05$.

T-test: A parametric test that determines the difference between two groups.

Two-tailed tests: Used to test nondirectional hypotheses.

Variability measures: Measures that characterize the variability of a set of scores, such as range, standard deviation, and variance.

Variance: The square root of the standard deviation.

10

Recording Media

In this chapter, I discuss different ways in which we can make a record of the observational data we sample. Thus, I use it differently than I used it in referring to recording rules in Chapter 6. In that earlier chapter, recording rules referred to those rules (i.e., 0/1, instantaneous, and continuous) that determined when we would recorded behaviors of interest. In this chapter, recording is used more literally to refer to the actual technology used in making physical records of the data. Physical records can be made, most basically, with paper and pencils or pens (such as checklists and narrative records) or with mechanical recording devices (such as audio and video recorders) and computerized event records. I make an effort to anchor these recording media to specific recording rules. These rules are displayed in Fig. 10.1.

The choice of a recording medium, like the choice of a category system and data analysis strategies, should be specific to the questions posed by the observer. Furthermore, simplicity is again preferred to complexity. You should choose a recording medium only as complex as needed to answer your specific question(s). Complexity of recording media, like complexity of data analysis strategies, does not make the project more sophisticated. Sophistication hinges on the type of question asked, not the technology used to answer it.

With this said, I begin by reviewing the simpler media, those techniques that use paper and pencil or pen, and then move onto mechanical and computer media.

PAPER AND PENCIL AS A RECORDING MEDIUM

The paper and pencil (or pen) recording media I discuss include narrative recording and checklists.

Narrative Systems

Narratives are descriptions of behaviors that include some reference to the ways in which the behaviors unfold across time. The duration of the description can vary

Technology	Recording Rules		
	Continuous	*0/1*	*Instantaneous*
Narrative	X		
Checklist	X	X	X
Tape recorder	X		
Videocamera	X		
Computerized event sampler	X	X	X

FIG. 10.1   Recording rules for recording media.

from one event las short time, such as a description of a child walking from the school bus into the classroom, to a more prolonged event, such as a description of a dinnertime conversation among family members. Generally, narrative descriptions provide detailed descriptions of what has been observed. From this description, categories can be derived, counted, and analyzed.

Just as the length of the event described can vary, so too can the level of specificity of the narratives. In some cases, the observer may use very specific language to describe specific behaviors that are relevant to the study. For example, if we were to use narrative recording for describing children's bouts of aggression on the playground, we might use continuous recording rules and use a specific list, or dictionary, of behaviors to describe such events. Furthermore, our a priori theory would have us focus on such things as the identity of the participants, their roles (e.g., initiator or reactor, superordinate or subordinate roles), and the outcome (e.g., benefits accrued).

In other cases, narrative descriptions can be more general. Although human observers selectively process information, we can construct narrative records that are rather more open-ended. For example, in the initial stages of conducting an observation (e.g., the entering the field stage) general descriptions about the activities on the playground could be recorded. Such a general description could later be used to generate more specific observational categories.

Evertson and Green (1986) suggested ways of differentiating among different forms of narrative recording systems. These (displayed in Table 10.1) include diary or journal records, critical incidents, specimen records, and field notes.

Diary or journal entries can be very general or more specific forms of narrative descriptions in which observers write their recollections of events after they have left the field. Diaries have a long and noble history in child study and psychology and are typically used in longitudinal research designs. For example, Darwin (1877) kept a diary of his son, as have an array of child psychologists (though many of them had daughters): Piaget (1962), Sachs (1980), Snow (1983), and Tomasello (1993). In both this chapter and the next chapter, on indirect observational methods, diary/journals are discussed. The interested reader should, thus, consult both chapters.

TABLE 10.1
Types of Narrative Systems

Type	Definition	Example
Diary/journal	Retrospective record of events	Mother's daily entries of baby's language
Critical incident	Record details of particular event	Describe aggressive bout
Specimen record	Details of a specific time period	Describe a school day
Field notes	Complete written records of ethnographer	Field entry notes

Parents who are not researchers but who are interested in their children's development also use diaries, often in a more general form. Parents' use of the diary method often takes the form of the baby diary. These often commercially prepared diaries typically are presented in different formats, such as the daily entry calendar format displayed in Fig. 10.2, or a landmark format where important events, such as first words, first steps, and so on are entered. In both cases but especially in the calendar format, we have an excellent record when something occurred, particularly if parents know what to look for; that is, parents can become reliable and valid observers of behavior if they have specific behaviors to record. The particulars of diary entries that maximize objectivity are discussed later in this section. As I discuss in Chapter 11, parents can keep diaries and logs that provide important information about how children spend their days. Such data are very important to the extent that they provide descriptions of what children spend their out-of-school time doing. Collection of this sort of data is neither very expensive nor very obtrusive; thus, diaries and logs are reasonable alternatives to direct observations.

Parental diaries, when complemented with other relevant pieces of information, can provide interesting information about children's development. Children's artifacts, such as artwork or writing samples, can provide interesting complementary information to diary entries. For example, a systematic record of children's early writing on a computer can easily be kept if parents note the date of various children's products. In this way, a permanent and dated longitudinal sample of writing is kept. Similarly, most parents save their children's report cards and favorite pieces of art and writing. Together with diary entries, such child artifacts can provide parents and others with systematic information on children.

For the researcher, diary information can also be an important source of information that might not be otherwise available. Data derived from diaries can be very informative to the extent that they are collected by someone close to the subject (usually a caregiver), are collected unobtrusively, and are privy to the most private moments of the participants. The last feature necessitates that the researcher treat diary data with the utmost respect and confidentiality. Additionally, diary data can be further complemented with any other sorts of data, such as artifacts, behavioral observations, psychometric measures, and so on (Braunwald & Brislin, 1979).

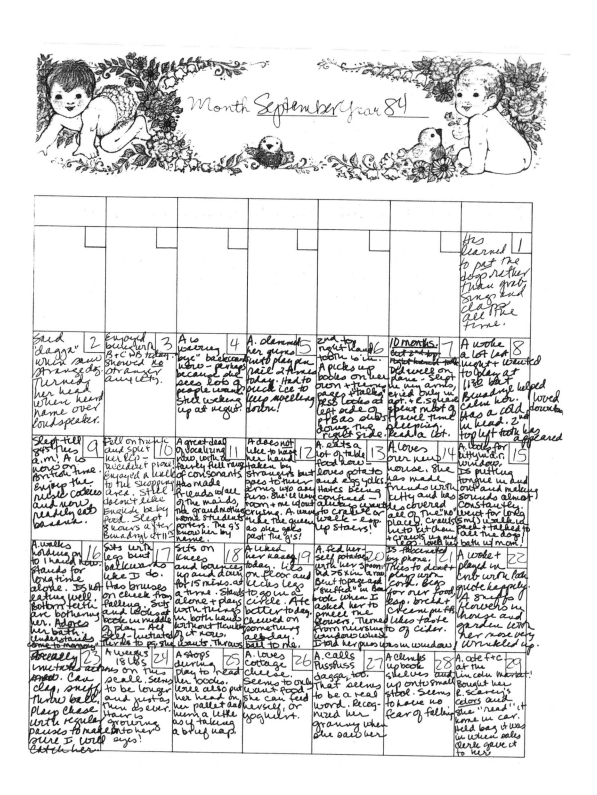

FIG. 10.2.   Calendar diary.

Those sources that complement a diary study, as well as the design of the diary per se, are determined by the function the diary is to serve and the specific question for which it will provide information. Diaries can be used as part of a research design either to generate or to test hypotheses. Correspondingly, diaries can be the prime or a complementary source of data. However, if diaries are to be used in research they must be designed with specific questions in mind (see Pellegrini, Galda, Shockley, & Stahl, 1995, for an example of diaries used in the study of literacy development).

Diaries can be used in a general way, to generate hypotheses, then in more specific ways. I used a diary method at the beginning of an observational research project. The diary data I collected were to provide the basis for a behavioral coding system, focal children to observe, and hypotheses. Data for these summaries were gathered while I was serving two roles. First, I was a parent helping to ease my son's transition into a new school in a foreign country; second, I was entering the field of the site for a new research project. During this time I observed all children, learned their names, and played with them on the playground. When I went home (after play time) I wrote these summaries. They became an important base for my identification of focal children and a behavioral coding system that would be subsequently field tested.

My entries were rather informal to the extent that there was no set format. Having a set format helps guard against some of the many pitfalls of the diary method: unreliability, selective attention, and other forms of bias (more limitations are discussed at the end of this section).

Braunwald and Brislin (1979) offered some excellent suggestions for the design of diary formats to minimize some of these problems. First, they recommended that diary formats should be double entry formats. That is, the same sorts of information should be listed in multiple locations in the diary. In this way, we have a measure of the reliability of the entry. Of course, what you record depends on your question but, by way of illustration, Braunwald and Brislin (1979) suggested the following categories for the study of early language development: Under the category *acts of communication,* or the actual utterances generated by a child, they differentiate among situations in which the child initiates or responds to a preceding utterance. For context they included the specific idea that the child is expressing, what prompted this expression, and whether the child acts as if he or she understands speech. For accompanying behaviors and reactions, they included gestures of the subject and interlocutors, information on the child's mood and voice tone, and information regarding the child's and interlocutors' failure to respond.

Second, they recommended a standard notation system to be used when making entries. For example, standard abbreviations and symbols should be used. It is also useful to include a glossary for these symbols and their operational definitions so that their consistent use is maintained. Last, they recommended maintaining a place in both the diarist's mind and in the format of the diary for unusual events, such as if the child chooses to use an unusual word rather than a more conventional one.

Figure 10.3 shows a diary format used with young adolescents. Time of the day is specified, as are actors and specific word choices. This sort of format is particularly useful where we want to make a comparison across different children on similar constructs. In this case I was studying bully–victim relationships.

Either time-based or event-sampling rules can be used for diaries. That is, entries can be made daily or weekly or they can be made after the occurrence of targeted events. Braunwald and Brislin (1979) recommended that diarists summarize their records monthly, in narrative form. This exercise, they argued, provides a useful abstract for the month's events and also may provide an opportunity for embellishing earlier entries.

It is also useful for the researcher to collect the diaries after summary points. Routine collection, particularly if the interval is relatively short, such as every few days or weekly, serves the dual functions of facilitating compliance by the diarists and minimizing the likelihood of losing the diaries. When these rules are followed, diaries

Date_____ Homeroom_____

Who'd you talk with today and where'd you talk with them?

_____ Who _____ Where _____

1.
2.
3.
4.
5.

What did you do and say to them? (Use the glossary.)

Did you hit or tease anyone? Who? How? (Use the glossary again.)

Where'd this happen?

Why'd you do it?

About how many other kids were around?

Who?

Did anyone hit or tease you? Who? How? (Use the glossary again.)

About how many kids were around?

Who?

How did you and they feel after?

Glossary: Doing nothing/unoccupied, near but not with someone, talk, argue, tease, tease back, rough play, fight/hit, fight/hit back, sad, happy, hurt, give up.

FIG. 10.3   Student diary.

can provide a very useful and objective data source for phenomena that might otherwise be very difficult or impossible to collect.

There are obvious advantages and disadvantages to diary and journal records. The main advantage is that it is relatively easy. It can be done after leaving the hustle and bustle of the field. The disadvantages are equally obvious. First, is the problem of a selective memory. That the data are recorded after the fact means that records may be reflecting what the observer chose to remember. This may be different from what actually occurred. Correspondingly, the problem of observer bias is an issue. Bias can be realized in what one chooses to remember and record. A diary may also be a record of what the participant intended to do rather than what he or she actually did. For example, British academics have used the records kept in their daily calendars to document their work load (*Times Higher Education Supplement*, 12 November 1993, *1097*). The entries may reflect what one hopes to do, in addition to what actually gets done! On the whole, however, diary methods are useful if observers try to check our biases. Finally, diaries are particularly useful for the entering the field stage of a project.

Critical incident recording is a form of narrative system similar to event or behavior sampling (cf. Chapter 6). In such cases, observers wait until a critical event occurs (e.g., aggression) and then record all the information that they see as relevant. As noted in the example earlier in this chapter and in the discussion of event sampling in Chapter 6, our theory of the meaning of the event will determine what we record. Generally, we want to record the full event from beginning to end and to note relevant behaviors (e.g., punch, kick), information about participants (e.g., names, number, and gender), structure (e.g., roles of key participants), and the consequence of the event (e.g., it ends when Sam runs away).

The problem with using paper and pencil to record complex events is speed, or more accurately, lack of speed. Writing takes lots of time relative to other recording media, and we may miss or omit important information as we attempt to have the pencil keep up with rapid events. One way in which this has been addressed is for observers to observe for a specified time, say 10 seconds, and then record for another specified time, another 10 seconds. There are other problems related to trying to write in places where we do not have a stable surface (such as on the playground, following children) or during bad weather. Writing is difficult if not impossible in cold and wet weather. A solution to these problems, discussed in more detail later in this chapter, involves having observers talk into microphones attached to small tape recorders. This method bypasses most of the limitations of paper and pencil.

The next narrative system, specimen records, like critical incidents can be more efficiently executed by talking into a tape recorder. Specimen records are tied to the tradition of ecological psychology pioneered by Barker and colleagues (e.g., Barker, 1968; Barker & Wright, 1955; Gump, 1989; Wright, 1960). Generally, specimen records are continuous, sequential recordings that occur in specific situations (Wright, 1960). Advocates of this approach suggest that observers record "everything," (Wright, 1960, p. 83) that occurs in a specific situation. As noted throughout this book, we cannot possibly record "everything" so we try to record what we see as relevant to our specific question.

Observers should begin by recording a description of the scene (e.g., a specific classroom), the participants, and their ongoing actions and language. For example, a specific child or other participant is chosen and observed in a theoretically relevant situation, such as in a child-care center. Descriptions are recorded in narrative form and should be objective to the extent that physical actions, such as twitching, and exact verbalizations of participants are recorded. Observers should record everything relevant to the question that is done by and to the focal participant. A time dimension should also be recorded. When separate narratives are cobbled together, they should form a diary-like collection, albeit a diary specific to a certain location, for a specific child; this record is the specimen record for the child (Wright, 1960). An example of a hypothetical specimen record is displayed next.

7:05 am: Anna (A), lying on her stomach in bed, looks up at her father (F), who is sitting on the bed next to her. A rubs her right eye with her right hand, then smiles broadly at F. F then bends over and kisses A on the left cheek. A continues to smile as F says "Good morning." A responds, "Good morning. Is today a school day?" F says "Yes." A sits up with crossed legs, yawns, and says, "Can we go to the pool after school?" F hesitates and says, "Mom's picking you up; let's go ask her." A stands on bed, jumps to floor, and runs into dining room calling "Hey Mom, can we go to the pool after school today?" Mom (M), sitting at the table, reading newspaper, eating cereal, looks up with a broad smile. M puts down paper, turns to face A with open arms and says, "Good morning, honey."

This hypothetical example might be a specimen record for the way in which one child begins a school day. I mean this may be the first segment of a description that begins with wake-up and ends with the child's entry into the school building. More broadly, a specimen record might include the child's whole day, including home, school, and home after school.

Specimen records can be quantified in the following ways (Wright, 1960). First, prevalence of behavior, such as smile, cry, and run, expressed in Likert-like terms (e.g., *frequently, sometimes, infrequently*) can be determined by summing values and ratings across the whole specimen record. Frequencies can be derived in a similar fashion by counting occurrences of events across the record. Second, the specimen records can be segmented into time units, for example, 10- or 30-second intervals, and duration scores of particular behaviors and events can be derived. Frequency scores can be derived from records organized in this fashion, as can rate measures, that is, occurrence of behavior per time unit. Third, specimen records can be examined in terms of meaningful units, such as breakfast time or father–child reunions at school. These events can be examined in terms of frequency, duration, and co-occurrence of component behaviors such as the frequency of verbal protests, smiles, mutual gazes, waves. Events can also be examined in terms of structure, or the ways in which these components are organized into a meaningful whole. In the case of father–child reunions as a child is collected from school, we could describe the sequence of behaviors from the time father and child first see each other until they both leave the school. In such cases, the sequential probability of various combinations of behavioral units can be determined.

The major limitations to this approach include the impracticality and impossibility of recording everything. As noted at various points in this book, descriptions by their very nature are selective; it is simply not possible to describe everything. However when records are made via mechanical or computer recording devices (to overcome the burden of trying to record information that occurs too rapidly and in a complex format), they provide wonderful descriptions of children in specific contexts.

Field notes are the last type of narrative recording to be discussed. Again, this method has been discussed in great depth by ethnographic researchers (see Corsaro, 1981; Fine & Sandstrom, 1988; Patton, 1990), so I am brief here. Field notes refer to written observations that ethnographers collect as part of their field studies. Field notes are often written, but could be audio recorded if this is not too obtrusive. Like specimen records, field notes attempt to capture the nature and sequence of participants and their behaviors (Evertson & Green, 1986; Patton, 1990). Observers use field notes to record sequences of and participants in behaviors of interest in particular contexts. Field notes may be taken on children's linguistic and social behaviors during a whole school day (Corsaro, 1981) or taken on a particular portion of the school day. For example, field notes could be taken for a specific literacy learning event, like reading lessons (e.g., Au, 1980, cited in Evertson & Green, 1986). In any case, objective descriptions and, where appropriate, verbatim transcriptions or recordings of oral language are made.

In addition to recording actual behaviors, some ethnographers, like Corsaro (1981), suggest that field notes include personal, methodological, and theoretical notes (see Chapter 4 for a discussion of these terms and their use in preliminary observations). Like specimen records, field notes are complementary to other data sources, such as artifacts, interviews, records, and even photographs (see Mead, 1954, for an interesting example of the use of photographs). An example of field notes follows.

It is first thing in the morning and "Y'All Know What?" time has just begun. Jason shows and talks about his penny that was squished on a railroad track. Ami shows the story she wrote the day before, holding the book up for the class to see and moving it around the circle. She comments, "I was gonna write 'the end' but I didn't find out the words." Kimberly sounds out T H E E N D, and Betty says, "I'll help you." Ami ends with, "But I didn't have time to write it." Jenna tells a story about the sea, and Betty comments, "Oh, Jenna, you ought to write about that sometime." Jenay says she's going to have a party and puts a sign-up sheet on Betty's desk. Penyata tells an elaborate story full of "and thens" punctuated by the refrain, "Where's my bookbag?" uttered in a very dramatic voice. Betty chimes in, "You know what? It's neat to write stories with characters talking like that, like you really talk." Rick then tells his story, with sound effects, about swimming in a neighbor's pool. It's a very exaggerated, funny story that uses his own version of Penyata's book bag chant. Betty says, "Oh, what a tall tale that is!" She then turns to the group and asks, "Why do you like Rick's story?" Various children respond, "Because it was funny." Betty agrees and adds. "And he used sound effects." Jenay comments, "And he said 'Hey man.'" Betty adds, "Yes, he talked like people would, so that you can understand it. Rick took something that really happened to him, like he really went swimming, and put extra stuff in it and made it fun. I loved it. I loved everybody's stories. It was so fun to hear what you have to say. You're all so interesting" (Galda, Shockley, Pellegrini, & Stahl, 1995).

To conclude this section on narrative systems as recording media, I reiterate that narrative descriptions can probably be most accurately implemented when we use a medium other than paper and pencil, which is too time consuming. Narrative descriptions are useful ways to record the sequences of behaviors of specific actors in time and in specific locations. Narrative descriptions will be most objective when they are recorded on the spot, rather than after the observations, and when observers follow specific rules (e.g., sampling rules) to minimize bias. A cost associated with narrative systems is that, for quantitative analyses of data, data must be taken from the narratives and put into some category system before they can be analyzed. This is extremely time consuming. Narrative descriptions are often useful as part of the category generation process, during which observers deduce categories from larger data sets.

Checklists

Although the use of paper and pencil methods are cumbersome with narrative systems, they can be useful for observers using checklists. Checklists are particularly useful and economical for the observer who knows in advance exactly what he or she wants to measure. That is, checklists are useful if we have a category system already in place. Categories defined in checklists, like other dimensions of categorization and measurement, should be consistent with the question. Behaviors or categories used in checklists are rather specific and could represent a refinement of categories generated through previous narrative systems. In this chapter, checklists of the sort used for live observations are discussed. Other forms of checklists, used retrospectively, are discussed in the next chapter.

Checklists can be broadly defined as lists of behavior or categories that the observer checks if they are observed. Checklists are sometimes listed in textbooks with rating scales, another paper and pencil data collection method. Whereas checklists tell us whether a behavior occurred or did not occur, rating scales rate a behavior along a continuum. Frequently but certainly not always, rating tells us about occurrences across a large span of time; for example, a rating scale could be used to determine the extent to which a specific behavior occurs across a long duration. Checklists, as used in live behavioral observations, take individual samples across time intervals. The following two examples are illustrative of each, respectively:

Ex. 1 Hits: Yes/no

Ex. 2 Hits: Often, sometimes, never

Rating scales like this, in my opinion, should not be used for behavioral observation. They are more appropriate for parents and teachers to use in rating their general experiences with specific children across time. For example, rating scales are often used to measure children's temperament. This sort of scale is discussed in Chapter 11.

Checklists are used in time sampling to record (with instantaneous, 0/1, or continuous rules) live behavior. To this end, observers need some sort of timing device to tell them when to record the behaviors of interest. As noted in Chapter 9, this is easily accomplished by using a timed beeper that sounds at predetermined intervals. The time intervals are represented by the individual rows on the checklist. For readers interested in a more in-depth discussion of a checklist, see Hinde (1973) and Martin and Bateson (1993), the sources for this discussion. Designing a rating scale requires categories that we have identified through prior observation or through reading. (The process of generating categories was discussed in Chapter 5.) The number of categories included in a checklist, organized in columns, should be limited. The time intervals are represented in the rows of the sheet. Logistically, it makes sense to organize the columns so that co-occurring behaviors are contiguous. It may also be helpful to leave a few blank columns; one can be used for remarks by the observer and the others could be used for additional categories that may come to light during initial observations (Martin & Bateson, 1993).

According to Martin and Bateson (1993), checklists can be used with all three recording rules. They suggest placing a mark on the line for instantaneous sampling, a mark in the box for 0/1 sampling, and at each of the appropriate sample intervals for continuous recording. Observers can use different symbols as checks; for example, if more than one target is being observed, initials or numbers can be used as tallies; this has the added benefit of identifying the participant. Alternatively, behavioral categories can be differentiated by using a variety of codes instead of tallies. Such an example is displayed in Fig. 10.4. This example shows nine types of play in the columns; the first letter in each column (F, C, or D) corresponds to a type of play (i.e., functional, constructive, and dramatic play). The second letter refers to the social dimensions of each form of play: S, P, and I for solitary, parallel, and interactive.

In this example each child is observed alternatively, every 10 seconds; each 10-second interval is represented by a separate row. Within each cell or sample interval we code children by first initial in the cell corresponding to the form of play exhibited. Because 0/1 sampling was used, the initials were placed within the cell. In interval 9 a note is made that Anna's DI play has a rough dimension to it.

Clearly, checklists, are useful for collecting certain types of data. If we have a limited number of categories participants and want to maintain the sequential integrity of the data, checklists are a simple and useful medium. Quantities of checklists can be produced in advance at relatively low cost and time investment. In short, checklists are an underutilized but powerful data collection medium. Limitations of checklists become apparent when we have a number of different participants, a large number of categories, or possibly ambiguous categories that might require reviewing. In these cases, some form of mechanical or computerized medium may be more appropriate.

Children: Mary (M), Anna (A)
Date: June 10, 1993
Context: Blocks

FS	FP	FI	CS	CP	CI	DS	DP	DI	Remark
				M					
				A					
					M				
							A		
							M		
								A	
								M	
								A	R&T
						A			

FIG. 10.4.   Play checklist that notes participants.

MECHANICAL AND COMPUTER RECORDING MEDIA

In this section, I discuss two general types of recording media: mechanical media (specifically, audio recorders and video recorders) and computerized event recorders. Use of these media are most appropriate when there are numerous and complex categories and large amounts of data to be processed. Both forms of technology can be used in the service of 0/1, instantaneous, and continuous recording, although tape recorders and video cameras are probably most useful and practical for continuous recording schedules. Of course, the use of these systems depends on availability, cost, expertise of the data collector, and possible intrusiveness of the technology in the data collection site.

Fortunately, our current level of technology is very high and getting higher at an incredibly rapid rate. This rapid pace of technological advance has a direct effect on the cost, availability, and ease of use. Specifically, small portable audio recorders are readily available for less than $25, and individual tapes within 90-minute capacities are available for about $1.00. These simple machines can be used to record language or can be used by the observer in lieu of paper and pencil to describe chains of behavior. Similarly, video cameras are readily available at reasonable prices. A Sunday outing to a park in most cities or a visit to a school play will show the availability of various forms of portable video cameras: Many parents now carry these lightweight machines instead of the once common movie and still cameras. For less than $500, one can purchase a camera that is very portable and useful at recording both visual and audio material. An added benefit to the popularity of these machines is that they are probably less obtrusive in data collection sites. In the "old days," when a video camera was introduced into a classroom, it was a major event. Kids spent lots of time looking at the machine and wanting to see through it and to look at their own pictures. Now the ubiquity of various forms of video cameras seemingly makes them less obtrusive.

This is not to say that an observer with a videocamera is not obtrusive. It makes sense to have settling-in period for an observer and then another period after introduction of the equipment. The information initially collected with a tape recorder or a video camera may reflect the participants' interest in it; therefore, the data are not representative and probably should not be used in any analyses. An observer must judge when participants are used to the presence of equipment and then start data collection in earnest. It is probably the case that more time is needed when observing in nonpublic settings like homes and when observing cultural groups to which the observer does not belong. This obviously is a subjective decision and requires good judgment.

As noted in Chapter 4, there are useful guidelines to follow, such as trying to work with a member of the group under observation. This person can help to determine where to observe and ways to appear less obtrusive. Additionally, members of the group are invaluable as data collectors, hypothesis generators, and interpreters.

Tape Recorders and Video Recorders

Tape recorders are probably the most common, easiest, and most economical forms of technology that can be used in data recording. In this section, I discuss using tape recorders for narrative descriptions and for recording participants' language. The various methods for using tape recorders are displayed in Fig. 10.5.

As I have noted throughout this chapter, tape recorders are very useful for narrative descriptions by observers. If continuous recording is used with numerous codes, the observer can narrate descriptions into the tape recorder. This is a quick and rather unobtrusive way to collect information. As an example, I have used this method to record children's playground behavior. Following focal child sampling and continuous recording rules, I and my colleagues dictated children's behavior continuously into small microphones clipped to our collars. These microphones were connected to small tape recorders kept in our jacket pockets or clipped to belts. The language we used to describe children's behavior was based on a common dictionary of behavioral terms for playground behavior. All observers were trained to use these common terms to describe behavior.

We transcribed these recordings to coding sheets on which the order of specific behaviors was maintained. Then we entered the data onto a computer disk for analysis. Temporal information was also available from the tape recordings; we could enter a time sequence as data were transcribed.

Use	Means
Narrative descriptions	Observer describes into microphone
Participants' language	Remote microphones
	Radio microphones

FIG. 10.5   Uses of tape recorders.

I recently became aware of another way in which tape recorders can be used to record narrative descriptions. A PBS *Mystery* on television had a pathologist conducting a post mortem on a murder victim. He was dictating his observations during the examination into a tape recorder!

Tape recording continuous data, although simple in the recording stage, becomes very time consuming as we transform the data into a form that is readable by a computer for data analysis. Consider the time involved in retrieving information from the playground tapes, putting that information on sheets, and then putting it onto computer disks! If actual time is not important and we have few behavioral categories, checklists are much more economical. Another alternative to narrative descriptions into tape recorders is to use computerized event recorders; they are discussed later in this chapter.

Perhaps a more practical use for tape recorders is for recording language. Remote location tape recorders and radio transmitted tape recorders can be used to record verbal interaction in field and laboratory settings. In field settings, we can place tape recorders in a location such as on a chair under the dinner table or in a child's bedroom and let it run for a specified time. In other cases (e.g., Wells, 1985), tape recorders placed in specific remote locations begin at various random points in order to sample language. Observers or participants may operate the tape recorders (see Dunn, 1988; Tizard & Hughes, 1983), or the tape recorders may be voice activated. In laboratory situations, remote microphones are often placed around the room; for example, in many laboratory schools, microphones are suspended from the ceiling at various points in the classrooms. Remote microphones are most effective when we are interested in sampling the language of a particular location or setting, such as a dramatic play area, or for sampling individuals in circumstances in which they are confined to a specified area that can be recorded by the microphone (e.g., a tape recorder under the dinner table to record dinner conversation).

Tape recorders are less useful when participants can move about, often out of the range of microphones, or use low volume language, such as whispers and private speech. In such cases, radio transmitted microphones and tape recorders are useful. These small and rather inexpensive systems are particularly useful in situations for focal child sampling or continuous recording, in which participants are mobile. The systems include a small microphone (about 2") clipped on the participant's collar or vest and a small transmitter (about 3" x 5") placed in a pocket or vest. This battery-operated microphone transmits a radio signal to a receiver, which should be in the same room as the participant. To record the output, either a tape recorder or a video camera can be connected to the receiver. Each system (i.e., microphone or transmitter, and receiver) is programmed to operate at a specific FM frequency.

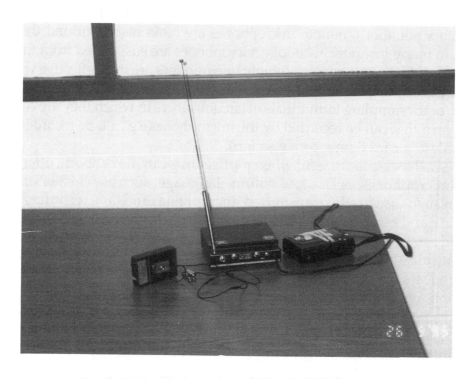

To record more than one person simultaneously, a researcher must program the systems at different frequencies; if not, the systems will jam each other.

More than one system is advised, in that it is time consuming to hook-up individual participants. It is more economical to record multiple participants simultaneously. Furthermore, unexpected breakdowns often warrant a back-up system. The cost of the systems (less than $100 each) makes them affordable.

Another useful hint for using radio microphones, particularly when they are used with a tape recorder rather than a video recorder, is to have a voice print of the focal person. When I use microphones with children, I first have them say their names and the day. In this way, I can more accurately discriminate their voices from the others they are talking with in the course of the observation.

With the recorded tapes in hand, the work continues. As with using tape recorders for narrative description, using recorders for language sampling can be very time consuming. It is particularly time consuming if tapes are transcribed verbatim. A rule of thumb is that transcription takes five or six times the recorded time. So if you have 1 hour of oral language, transcription should take 5 or 6 hours. More time is required if contextual information is included. When transcribing, it makes ultimate sense to use a transcription machine in that the pedal stop and go control allows the transcriber to write or type while stopping and advancing the tape. In short, it saves time in an already time-intensive enterprise. As with checklists, a researcher should decide how to code the language on the tapes and code from the tapes, foregoing the transcription. Rules similar to those outlined for narrative descriptions apply here.

Video recorders are useful in many of the same ways that tape recorders are useful. The added benefit of videocameras, of course, is that they provide not only audio but also visual data. This is particularly useful when we study social behavior, but it is also useful in the study of language, especially if we are interested in the context in which the language is used. For example, if we are interested in the language of children's play, it is imperative to tie the utterance to the gesture in order to make a reasonable inference about the meaning of the utterance. Take the utterance, "This is good." With a video recording we could see that the child is taking an empty spoon to his mouth and pretending to eat from it.

A problem often associated with the microphones attached to video recorders is that they are usually nondirectional and are thus relatively poor at recording conversations in a crowded room. This problem can be remediated, however, by connecting radio microphones to video cameras. In this way we can follow focal subjects with the video camera and simultaneously record their language and corresponding behavior.

Video recorders are also very useful in recording social behavior, particularly complex and rapidly occurring social behavior. For rather simple behaviors (i.e., few and simple codes), checklists probably are appropriate, but if there are numerous codes that require careful viewing and reviewing, video recording is essential. The videotaped incidents can be viewed repeatedly to assure coding accuracy. Again, the costs associated with viewing videotapes should be considered. Viewing tapes takes lots of time, certainly more time than would be involved in coding live behavior or in recording audiotapes. In some cases it might be better to code live with checklists, thereby economizing on time.

Video recording can help economize when a limited supply of observers is available to record behavior. If the location allows and research design permits, single observers can make videotapes of groups of individuals. The behavior of individuals within that group can later be coded from the videotapes.

Finally, video recorders are essential in training observers. In the initial stages of observer training, a large and varied behavioral sample is essential to set definitions of behaviors. For observers to record behaviors reliably, they should be trained on videotaped incidents of relevant behavior.

In short, tape recorders and video cameras offer relatively inexpensive means for recording behavior. Like other aspects of observational research, the method should be tied to the specific questions asked by the researcher. With this in mind, the researcher should choose a medium that most efficiently records his or her data.

Researchers should also consider using photographs to record important information. The use of photos to record important dimensions of children's development and culture was pioneered more than 50 years ago by Gregory Bateson and Margaret Mead. Photos can be useful in recording physical layouts of classrooms and playgrounds, as well as samples of children's work and many other things (see Mead, 1954, for some interesting examples).

Computer Event Recorders

Computer event recorders are more recent arrivals on the scene than are either tape recorders or video recorders. Consequently, they are more expensive and more complicated to use than tape recorders and audio recorders. Event recorders are microcomputers that the observer uses to record behavior in a form that is compatible with computers for subsequent data analyses; thus, all the costs associated with getting the data to that form are eliminated. This is no small saving. In my example of using tape recorders for narrative descriptions of playground behavior, the observers narrated descriptions in verbal form; these verbalizations were then put onto coding sheets, which were in turn entered onto computer disks. Event recorders could have been used: The observers could have entered the focal children's identification codes, their behaviors (and the duration of each), and their fellow interactants.

Event recorders save time over other methods. There are, however, time costs initially associated with event recorders: It take a fair amount of time to learn to use them. Another obvious cost is the computer itself. Hardware and software may be specifically designed for event sampling or a laptop or notebook can be used as an event recorder. Specifically designed event recorders are often smaller than laptops and sometimes include basic statistical packages for data analyses. The Observer is one such system, housed in a small (i.e., 8 x 14 x 3 cm, 250g) computer that costs somewhere around $2,000 (available from Noldus Information Technology b.v., University Business & Technology Centre, Varding 51, 6702 EA Wageningen, The Netherlands).

The Observer can handle up to 89 different events (i.e., categories) and their modifiers. Additionally, there are functions to identify location as well as the class of events and participants. Real time recording of events is also logged and accurate at the .1-second level. Basic statistical procedures, such as descriptive statistics and sequential analyses, are included. Reviews of this system have been written by Boccia (1992), Hille (1991), and Tourtellot (1992).

In evaluating a computerized event recorder, a few criteria are helpful (Martin & Bateson, 1993). The keyboard should be arranged such that a sufficient number of keys are available for different categories, with minimal use of function keys. Capacity should exist to design new programs should the extant programs not be adequate. Correspondingly, the computer should have an adequate number of set programs. Data should be easily stored, either on a diskette or on a hard drive, and the machine should have adequate memory. There should be a display system so that the user can confirm that the key pressed is the one wanted. Portability and dependability are also important. The weight, size, and battery life of the computer are important considerations, especially when observations are made in remote field locations. Finally, the machine should be dependable; if it is not, it is not worth using.

On the other hand, laptop computers can be used as event recorders by loading commercially prepared programs or programs prepared by academics. There are charges for the former class of programs, but there are typically not charges for the latter. For example, William Roberts at Cariboo College (Kamloops, British Columbia, Canada, V2C 5N3), has developed a program for the collection and analysis of observational data. To use such programs, users should contact the author for copies of the program and a manual; the programs typically cannot be used for commercial purposes.

The costs and benefits associated with computerized event recorders have been succinctly summarized by Martin and Bateson (1993). As already noted, the benefits include transforming data from either verbal descriptions or checklist formats into computer readable form; this is a real benefit because this process is very time consuming and prone to error. Furthermore, a rapidly occurring stream of behavior can be recorded, with an accurate record of the duration of events. Some of the costs associated with these machines are the expense and the time required to learn to operate the machine. Time must also be spent to check for recording errors; actually, an easy error detection procedure is a very important component of any recording system. Finally, computers sometimes malfunction and data can be lost; this is an obvious danger any time we use a computer. We must make sure that the program and the machine work so that we can avoid losing data.

SUMMARY AND CONCLUSIONS

In this chapter, I have discussed various media by which data can be recorded. The range of technology available is immense, spanning probably 200 years of technological development. We should not associate less technological forms, like checklists, with low levels of sophistication. Parsimony is a rule applied throughout this book: Use the simplest form of technology that will adequately do the job. On the other hand, if you have an interesting question that requires a computer event recorder, make the investments necessary to utilize that system. Again, the stress is on the question driving the technology.

THINGS TO THINK ABOUT

1. Utilizing a diary format (first general, then specific) keep track of some aspect of your family's life, such as affect at the breakfast table, dinner cooking, and cleanup routines, or parental uses of discipline strategies.

_____

_____

_____

_____

_____

_____

_____

_____

2. Try this again using written field notes.

_____

_____

_____

_____

_____

_____

_____

_____

3. Design a checklist to be used at home, school, or work. Have two codes: social and nonsocial. Use it to observe according to focal subject and scan sampling rule and 0/1, instantaneous, and continuous recording.

_____

_____

_____

_____

_____

_____

_____

_____

4. Use a write narrative system and then a tape-recorded narrative system to describe the behavior of a family event, say dinnertime or planning a trip. Which is easier? Which seems to be more obtrusive to the participants?

_____

_____

_____

_____

_____

_____

_____

_____

5. Try recording an event with a videocamera. Is this more or less obtrusive than talking into a tape recorder?

_____

_____

_____

_____

_____

_____

_____

_____

6. If you are contemplating the purchase of a computer event recorder, first try to operate a statistical package on a personal computer. The level of difficulty of this task is said to be equivalent to learning to use an event recorder.

_____

_____

_____

_____

_____

_____

_____

_____

GLOSSARY

Checklist: A paper and pencil method used to record occurrence and nonoccurrence of behaviors.
Give your example:

_____

_____

_____

_____

Critical incident: A form of narrative recording that describes a specific incident.
Give your example:

_____

_____

_____

_____

Diary method: A narrative method in which events and behaviors are recorded from memory.

Ethnography: A branch of anthropology that documents the daily life of a group from the perspective of the participants.

Field notes: Notes taken by ethnographers; they detail all relevant behavior and relationships.
Give your example:

_____

_____

_____

Key informant: A member of the group being studied who helps the researcher to understand the group better.
Give your example:

_____

_____

_____

_____

Likert scale: An ordinal response scale. For example: He's happy: (1) *Always;* (2) *Mostly;* (3) *Sometimes;* (4) *Not Often;* (5) *Never.*
Give your example:

_____

_____

_____

_____

Narrative system: Recording system in which events are described in a temporal context. Recording can be made live or from recall.

Radio microphone: A wireless microphone that transmits a voice to a tape recorder.

Rating scale: Scale in which behaviors typically rated across time are rated ordinally; see Likert.
Give your example:

_____

_____

_____

_____

_____

Recording media: Those forms of technology, such as tape recorders and check-lists, that are used to record behavioral data.

Specimen record: A form of narrative wherein the details of a specific time period (e.g., a children's school day) are described in great detail.
Give your example:

_____

_____

_____

_____

_____

11

Seeing Without Looking:
Indirect Data Collection Techniques

In this chapter, I discuss some ways to collect behavioral data indirectly. These techniques are in contrast to the direct observational techniques that have been discussed throughout most of this volume. Rather than relying on live observational techniques in the field, I explore some ways in which we can collect information without actually being in the field. These indirect techniques are particularly useful in collecting information about children and their families in nonpublic settings, such as in the home. Thus, these techniques are most usefully applied to situations where issues of logistics or economics (e.g., traveling to individual homes across a diverse area) or privacy-related concerns (e.g., the impracticality of being in homes during the early morning) prevent us from conducting direct observations. Instead, we rely on participants' immediate or recollected observations of behaviors of interest. The techniques discussed in this chapter include rating scales, remote or spot sampling, diaries, and remote tape recorders left at data collection sites. These indirect methods can be used either by themselves or in concert with direct observational methods. First, I discuss some general reasons to choose an indirect strategy over a more direct one.

WHY AND WHEN TO USE INDIRECT METHODS

Probably the most compelling reason to use indirect methods is that of economy. The process of observing individual children and families is exceptionally time consuming. A reliable behavioral sample of data requires numerous observations of each participant. These multiple observations of individual children in specific and sometimes difficult-to-reach settings must be multiplied by the number of participants we are studying. In short, direct observations are very expensive.

The amount of time invested can be diminished with some indirect methods, such as rating scales and spot sampling. For example, if we are interested in children's levels of social interaction or aggression, we could ask parents or teachers to rate the children on these dimensions, rather than conducting direct observations. The specific positive and negative aspects of such a technique are discussed in the section on rating scales; suffice it to say that a positive aspect of this approach is that a large number of participants can be surveyed in a short time relative to the time investment required for a direct observational study. An additional benefit of relying on information provided by a parent or a caregiver is that we can ask them questions that tap their more general knowledge of the child. That is, certain indirect methods, such as questionnaires, can be developed such that they ask informants to provide information on their general and varied experiences with the child. This contrasts with the more context specific information provided by direct observations; thus, indirect methods can provide information on general and diverse aspects of children's lives.

A second reason for using indirect methods is related to necessity more than to convenience. There are situations when we simply cannot conduct direct observations and, consequently, we must rely on indirect methods. These situations are those that are difficult to visit. The difficulty in access may be due to children being in remote locations; for example, a sample of children may be distributed across a large geographic area. Difficulty in access may also be due to participants' desire for privacy. For example, much of the bullying that takes places in schools occurs in bathrooms. We would have difficulty conducting direct observations there; thus, we must rely on indirect methods of the sort discussed in Chapter 10.

The following example illustrates the usefulness of indirect methods in this sort of situation. Consider a case in which we are interested in comparing the routines used by single parents and two-parent families in getting their children ready for school in the morning. It may be impossible for this to be directly observed. Answering such a question would involve observers going out to individuals' home on numerous occasions. On the privacy level, parents may be very reluctant to allow researchers into their homes during this part of the day. In short, to answer this question would require that we identify numerous volunteers who agreed to have us in their homes at a time that most parents rightly choose to keep private. One way around this obstacle is to ask parents to complete a rating scale of their morning routines. That is, we could design questions that we think are important to the morning routine and ask caregivers to complete them. This technique is explored in the next section on rating scales.

Another method that can be utilized is remote or spot sampling. Generally, remote sampling (Bloch, 1989) involves sampling participants' behaviors with either telephone contact or through the use of diaries or logs at specified time intervals. For morning routines before school, parents could be contacted by telephone and asked a series of questions about their morning routines. Alternatively, parents could enter in diaries or logs, at predetermined times, aspects of their morning routine (Pellegrini et al., 1995). Figure 11.1 shows a diary used for this purpose in the study of children's literacy practices at home.

More directly, parents could switch on an audio recorder, placed in a central location, to record the interaction. Remote sampling seems to represent an intermediate step between direct observations and rating scales completed in the absence of an observer.

CHILD'S NAME:

YOUR NAME:

DATE: 2-1-95

RELATIONSHIP WITH CHILD: Mother

Please complete information ONLY for today.

	WITH WHOM	WHERE	HOW LONG
THIS MORNING			
Look at books: yes / no	Mother	At home	20 min
Pens/Pencils/Crayons, etc.:	Sister and mother	At home	10 mine
Played: games	Mother and Brother and sister	At home	30 min
What did they play: Read Book	Mother and Brother and sister	At Home	20 min
AFTER SCHOOL TODAY			
Look at books: yes / no	Mother and Sister	At home	25 min
Pens/Pencils/Crayons, etc.:	Sister	At home	15 min
Played: games	Mother and sister and Brother and Friends	At Home	1 hour
What did they play: BasketBall	Brother and sister and Friends	At home	1 hour
THIS EVENING			
Look at books: yes / no	Sister	At Home	30 min
Pens/Pencils/Crayons, etc.:	Sister and mother	At Home	15 min
Played: games	Brother and sister and Friends	At Home	45 min
What did they play: Kick Ball	Brother and sister and Friends	At home	45 min

FIG. 11.1.   Home literacy diary.

RATING SCALES

Rating scales enable observers, be they external observers, participants themselves, or people close to the participants, to rate the degree to which specific behaviors or characteristics exist. Rather than indicating presence or absence of a behavior (which is accomplished by checklists), rating scales are measures of degree. Consider asking a teacher to rate the degree to which a child concentrates on seat work. A rating scale item for this might take the following form:

Concentrates on seat work

1   2   3   4   5

Never   Always

Different forms of rating scales are outlined in greater detail later in this section.

Another characteristic of the rating scale method is that it can be completed by an external observer, such as an observer in the field, who rates specific aspects of the environment or behavior. Thus, this method can be used in some of the same ways as a checklist. Examples of rating scales scored by external observers include the measures of home environments developed by Betty Caldwell and Robert Bradley (1984) and Theodore Wachs (1985). With each of these techniques, the observer enters the home of the participant with a detailed rating scale for aspects of the home physical environment (e.g., the number of newspapers and magazines in the home) and the social environment (e.g., the degree to which caregivers respond to a child's cries of distress). The external observer can complete the rating scale items either at predetermined intervals while observing in the home or after leaving the site. The first case is a form of time sampling with direct observation whereas the second case uses recollection.

In other cases, rating scales can be completed by a participant in the field, such as a parent, a teacher, or a classmate of a focal child. Measures of children's temperament are good examples of the sort of rating scale for which a parent or a teacher is asked to rate children on a number of dimensions, such as activity level and flexibility. Rating scales have been developed for teachers to use as part of the process of diagnosing and treating children with problems. For example, Rutter (1967) developed a rating scale for teachers to rate children on behaviors such as nail biting and hitting, which may demonstrate, respectively, neurotic and antisocial dimensions of children's personality.

When rating scales are completed by a participant in the field, ratings are often based on recollections, rather than time sampled observations. Consequently, the scores generated by these scales represent rather global ratings of children, probably based on long and repeated observations. There are obvious costs and benefits associated with each method of implementing these forms of rating scales. Specifically, a real benefit corresponds to the economy of data collection. By having a number of participants completing rating scales, we save on the numerous hours that would be required to collect this information directly.

The costs associated with rating scales and questionnaires completed by participants are obvious. The first limitation is that participants' responses may be influenced by the social desirability of certain responses. By this I mean that when participants are asked to comment on their children or their parenting, they often respond in such a way that they tell us what they think is expected of them rather than what they actually do. For example, if we ask parents about their uses of corporal punishment with children, their responses may be influenced by what they think we approve of. This sort of problem has been documented in some of the early studies of child socialization (Sears, Maccoby, & Levin, 1957).

Another well-documented and related problem associated with participant-completed rating scales is the effect of the recency of memory. There is a tendency for respondents to record the most recent behaviors rather than those that are the most representative. For example, when asked about parental disciplinary strategies, parents may record their latest techniques rather than ones they have used for a longer period of time. Similarly, parents may record some events because they are more memorable than others, even though they may be less representative. For example, if asked about children's sleeping habits, parents may stress the more memorable patterns, such as early morning waking.

A number of these limitations are minimized when external observers and time sampling strategies are used. Specifically, problems of selective memory and recency of memory for certain events or behaviors are minimized by systematic sampling strategies. Sampling, as discussed previously, minimizes these problems by choosing systematically across various periods. Again, the associated cost of observers spending the time in the field necessary to obtain an adequate sample is a nontrivial consideration.

The long-term knowledge that caregivers have of their children can, however, be used to the advantage of the observer. Having well-informed raters draw on their long and varied relationships with participants can be invaluable. That is, scores generated by these raters could represent numerous and varied sampling points, rather than the more limited sampling points of an external rater. Consequently, the ratings may be very stable and accurate indicators of a trait or behavioral tendency. This may be particularly true for rare behaviors. For example, if we are interested in children's imaginary playmates, parental reports may be excellent indicators to the extent that parents probably witness numerous episodes as they occur in different but limited settings. The scores are valid if the previously mentioned limitations, such as recency and social desirability, are minimized. After I discuss different types of rating scales, I outline some ways to minimize some of the problems inherent in rating scales.

Five types of rating scales including numerical, graphic, standard, cumulated points, and forced choice scales, have been suggested (see Fig. 11.2).

The numerical rating scale can take different forms, but it generally has the rater assigning a numerical value to a descriptor, such as the one given earlier in this section. Alternatively, individual descriptors representing dimensions of a trait can be listed, and the rater could score one of those rather than assigning a number to some descriptor the rater thinks the number may represent. An example of this sort follows:

Type	Definition
Numerical	Numbers assigned to a descriptive sequence
Graphic	Descriptors on a linear array
Standard	Rated against standardized criteria
Cumulated points	Sum of scores in categories
Forced choice	One choice descriptor

FIG. 11.2   Types of rating scales.

Concentrates on seat work

1. Never settles into the tasks.
2. Begins task, then loses interest after short while.
3. Works through until encounters difficulty.
4. Works through unless interrupted by another.
5. Works through beginning to end almost always.

The probable benefit of this form of item is that it is explicit. The rater is told precisely what each number represents. In the scale example presented previously, the rater assigns his or her own meaning to each category. This ambiguity is usually not problematic in extreme categories, such as 1 and 5 ratings, but for the rest it is. The meaning that I assign to a 3 or a 4 may be very different from the meaning you assign to them. Thus, rating scales that have verbal descriptors next to each value are more likely to be reliable than those without the descriptors.

Graphic representations of rating items merely represent the choices outlined for numerical systems along a horizontal or vertical line. An example of a graphic representation of a numerical rating scale is provided.

Concentrates in class

1	2	3	4	5
Never	Seldom	Sometimes	Frequently	Always

The third type of rating scale, according to Guilford (1953; as cited in Irwin & Bushnell, 1980), is a standard type. The rating is against some standard criterion, such as percentage. The following example shows a scale for rating one student's ability to concentrate compared to other students.

Concentrates

TOP 5%   TOP 10%   TOP 25%   TOP 33%   AVERAGE   LOWER 33%

The fourth type of rating scale is a cumulative type. The rater, instead of scoring one response to a question, scores as many descriptors as are relevant. For example, a program evaluator many be interested in the extent to which different teachers implement specific program components. Rating scales could be constructed such that each question corresponds to a component and the rater scores the number of components that are implemented. Such an example is presented here.

Individualized instruction:

___Children work at different rates
___Children do work for different subjects at different times.
___Children choose their own reading books.
___Children choose topics for reports.

Scores for each item would be the sum of criteria met.

A related form of cumulative rating is the *guess who description.* In this case the responder is presented with a list of descriptors, and he or she must name a participant who best fits the descriptor. This type of rating scale item is currently being utilized in the childhood aggression literature. Teachers and children are given descriptions such as, "He always is fighting. He bullies weaker children in class."

Finally, we have the forced choice rating scale (Guilford, 1954, as cited in Irwin & Bushnell, 1980). Rather than having numerous criteria on which to rate participants, scorers must choose only one. An example of this sort of item is presented here.

During recess he/she:

___Keeps to himself/herself.
___Plays with one or two children.
___Plays in large groups.
___Involved in aggressive episodes.

As I noted previously, rating scales in their different forms have advantages and disadvantages. Many of the disadvantages relate specifically to the ways in which the scales are constructed. Thus, to maximize their utility we should design rating scales such that the weaknesses are minimized.

A basic problem with many rating scales, alluded to in the previous discussion, is that some rating scale items can be very ambiguous. For example, when we are asked to rate someone on a scale from 1 to 5, we should be given specific criteria, whether they be verbal descriptors or numerical standards, to use as guides.

Another important issue relates to who completes the rating scales, especially in cases where raters are data collectors rather than participants. In the discussion of observer bias, I suggested that biases about certain participants may color the way in which they are rated. For example, if one data collector spent time observing children on the playground at recess for many weeks, he or she probably has a good sample of children's social behavior and social skills and probably has formed specific beliefs and attributions about those children. If that data collector were to complete a rating scale on the same children's behavior in the classroom, the knowledge of those children on the playground might contaminate the classroom ratings. Thus, different observers should conduct different data collection procedures. In this way we minimize bias. The bias holds true for raters and interviewers who then serve as observers; the information from the interviews influences the way in which they code their observations.

In order to maximize the benefits inherent in rating scales used by teachers, it makes good sense to give them the rating scales after they have had time to get to know the children. As a rule of thumb, I do not ask teachers to complete rating scales on children until after Thanksgiving. Furthermore, they should have adequate time to familiarize themselves with the instrument and enough time to complete it. Specifically, teacher should read over the instrument thoroughly, observe the child with the items from the instrument in mind, and then complete the scale. Allowing enough time for rating scales to be completed helps to minimize inaccurate completion. Often in the hurry to complete a large number of long questionnaires, raters do a hurried and sometimes inaccurate job. Another way to minimize this is to offer some compensation for their time. For example, money, classroom supplies, and children's books are often greatly appreciated by busy teachers who take time to help.

Finally, like most data collection techniques, rating scales are probably best used in concert with other types of measures, such as behavioral observations and psychometric measures. The different techniques typically complement each other. Cairns and Cairns (1986) suggested that behavioral observations provide normative data on participants, whereas rating scales completed by teachers and parents, even when they are centered on the same phenomena, often give information about children's individual differences. Thus, together, the two techniques give us a fairly complete picture.

Rating scales can also be used as complements to direct behavioral observations. For example, rating scales could be used to help observers locate where and when certain behaviors or sets of behaviors occur. Further, in using certain types of questionnaires, we can find out the specific times and places that behaviors of interest occur. Using a form of cumulated points scale, we can locate where young children learn certain types of mathematics:

Rank the situations in terms of frequency in which counting games occur:

___In the bath.
___At bedtime.
___Watching Sesame Street.
___Setting the table.
___Walking up and down stairs.

Based on the information gathered from this sort of question, observers could then conduct direct observations of the relevant situations. In this way observers' time can be used most efficiently because they are in the field observing relevant phenomena; the extent to which they are spending time waiting for something to happen is minimized. See Pellegrini and Stanic (1993) for an outline of specific cases in which questionnaire data are used to locate relevant behavioral events to be observed.

REMOTE SAMPLING

In this section, I discuss remote, or spot, sampling. This data collection technique is most useful in circumstances in which it is very difficult and obtrusive for an external observer to conduct direct observations. Generally, this method involves a participant in the field recording what he or she is doing at predetermined sampling intervals. The recording can be done in a diary or in response to questions asked by a telephone interviewer. It has been used most fruitfully by researchers who have been interested in what children do at home. These researchers (e.g., Bloch, 1989; Csikszentmihalyi, 1990; Pellegrini & Stanic, 1993) were interested in how children spent their time while they were in situations that were difficult for external observers to observe. Logistically and economically, it is very difficult and expensive for observers to follow participants in their everyday routines. Remote sampling provides an interesting alternative method to direct observation. In the example that follows, I illustrate how it can be implemented.

Recently George Stanic and I (Pellegrini & Stanic, 1993) proposed the necessity of describing the ways in which preschool children from different groups within the U.S. come to construct mathematical concepts. In order to understand this process, we proposed describing children's *developmental niche,* as discussed by Super and Harkness (1986). The developmental niche is a description of the ways in which cultural knowledge, such as mathematics, develops in children. To this end, it is imperative to provide descriptions of the physical and social dimensions of children's everyday lives. In reality, this means following children as they make the rounds of their daily lives, often moving to a number of different locations. Additionally, descriptions of the participants and the processes characterizing these different settings are important. Thus, remote sampling is a good candidate for this job that is all but impossible to execute with direct observational measures.

Methodologically, the data can be collected on children's everyday experience in the following ways. We begin with a series of research questions. These questions should be translated into a series of questions that can be presented in either telephone interview form or that can be written in a diary or log. In our work on locating mathematical competence we proposed having telephone interviewers call children's caregivers at predetermined intervals to ask them the questions that are listed in Fig. 11.3. We used a time sampling strategy, implemented with telephone interviewing, to determine where children were, with whom and with what they were interacting, and the processes that characterized these settings.

Other researchers, such as Tamis-Lemonde, Kahana-Kalman, Damast, and Bornstein (1992), have also used telephone interviews to sample children's development in their everyday context. Specifically, Bloch (1989) used telephone interviews to ask caregivers to describe the physical locations of their young children's play at home. She described the degree to which young boys and girls played in the home, yard, or neighborhood. Kahana-Kalman, Tamis-Lemonde, and Bornstein (1992) used telephone interviews to

Spot Observation Form

Focal Child_____ Caller_____

_____ Date_____ Time_____

CALL: Original   Callback 1   Callback 2   RESPONSE:

    Yes   No

QUESTIONS: (Write responses and additional prompts used.)

Where is [name of focal child]?

Can you see him/her?

Whom is [name of focal child] with? [Determine ages and relationships.]

What is [name of focal child] doing? OR What are they doing? What objects is

[name of focal child] using? What is [name of focal child] saying?

Is he/she using numbers or counting?

    How?

Is he/she playing with a number/counting games?

    Which one?

Is he/she engaging in make-believe using numbers/counting?

    How?

Is he/she looking at a number book?

    Which one?

Is he/she writing numbers?

    How?

FIG. 11.3.   Questions for telephone interview.

collect data on the language development of toddlers. Interviewers called the homes of focal children weekly and asked parents a series of questions about children's language development. For example, to investigate children's word comprehension and production, interviewers read mothers lists of specific words and phrases and asked if the child understood or used them.

In a further effort to standardize the responses of different people, it is reasonable to provide a glossary of words to be used in completing the diary. This practice was illustrated in the preceding chapter.

Another way in which remote sampling can be implemented is through the use of diaries or logs, rather than (or in some cases in addition to) telephone interviews. Diaries or logs, as discussed in Chapter 10, are most useful and reliable when specific descriptors or questions are used to organize respondents' entries. If specific questions are asked, we have a standardized and systematic procedure by which we can aggregate our data.

Logistically, diaries can be implemented in at least three ways. First, the can be retrospective recollections of key events or behaviors. For example, at the end of each day or at the end of each week primary caregivers could enter relevant information. Second, entries could be made contemporaneously; that is, entries could be made when critical events, such as the use of a specific word or phrase, occur. Third, entries could be made on a time sampling schedule: At predetermined intervals respondents would make entries. These predetermined intervals can be marked by using electronic beepers, as were used by Csikszentmihalyi (1990) in his studies of adolescence. A less expensive alternative to programmable beepers is the use of inexpensive digital watches with alarm functions (I thank Doug Kleiber for this suggestion). These watches (about $30) can be programmed to so that an alarm sounds daily at specific points. At those points, respondents make their diary entries. In this way we have a time sample of children's activities. Of course, these diaries then must be collected and summarized at reasonable points. As noted in Chapter 10, it probably makes sense to collect them weekly so that loss can be minimized.

The final remote sampling technique discussed in this chapter involves the use of remote tape recorders. With this technique a tape recorder is left in one location to record the interactions of participants. Variations on this technique were used successfully by Dunn (1988) in studies of sibling interaction, Tizard and Hughes (1983) in their longitudinal study of home–school relations, and Wells (1985) in his studies of language use in the homes of families from different social economic addresses. Most simply, this technique involves leaving a tape recorder always running in one location. Obviously, the choice of the location in which the recorder is left is critical. It should be left in an area in which the relevant type of interaction will occur. For example, language researchers interested in children's monologues or in discussions with siblings have frequently left tape recorders in children's bedrooms. Parents are typically asked to insert tapes and engage the recorder. Tapes, like diaries, are collected at regular intervals.

More technologically sophisticated is the use of the voice activated tape recorder. These tape recorders are left in a specified location; they engage automatically when voices are detected and disengage when there is silence. The benefits of this sort of machine over the manually operated recorders are unclear. On the one hand, we are saving a step by having the machine engage automatically. The corresponding benefit is that the machines probably are less reactive to the participants, and consequently the recorded data are probably more representative than those recorded with manually operated machines. The down side of the automatic machines may be that participants forget to change tapes or that data collectors have to go around to the sites to change and collect tapes at regular intervals. Of course, voice-operated recorders are also more expensive than the manual versions.

Another form of expensive but nice technology is a tape recorder that automatically engages at predetermined sampling points (e.g., for 15 minutes every day). This sort of technology, used very effectively by Wells (1985), relies on time sampling strategies to collect systematic oral language samples. Again, tapes are collected and distributed on a regular basis, like diaries. The reader interested in these techniques is referred to Wells (1985), where the methodology and logistics are fully described.

Recording oral language of this sort provides lots of, and often too much, data. Indeed, one must be selective about the ways in which the data are used: It is a daunting task to transcribe and code the tapes. If you know what you are looking for, by all means, code the language directly from the tapes. Transcription is incredibly time consuming. If, on the other hand, you are unclear about the coding scheme to be used, transcription may help you to design one, but recognize the large time investment.

Another issue to consider when using remote tape recorders is the obvious lack of context provided. That is, tape recorders record sounds and only sounds. Thus, we do not know about the corresponding actions, locations, or materials that accompany the utterances.

SUMMARY AND CONCLUSIONS

In this chapter, I outlined some ways in which we can "see" phenomena that are often hidden from observers. They are hidden because they often are embedded in the private lives of those we wish to study. Because they are difficult to access, more indirect methods are called for. I outlined a variety of techniques, ranging from direct observations by external observers using rating scales to more indirect methods such as diaries and telephone interviews. As noted throughout this book, different data sources are often complementary; that is, different techniques often provide a slightly different look at the phenomena of interest. Thus, where possible the researcher should use a variety of techniques. For example, if we are interested in studying the ways in which children's mathematical knowledge develops at home before school, we might begin by using telephone interviews to determine the time and location of those events that are most relevant to our question. Then we should probably spend time in those specific settings collecting direct observational data as well as in-depth diary or interview data.

THINGS TO THINK ABOUT

1. What are some criteria that could be the basis for designing a rating scale to study aspects of children's social competence (such as cooperation, aggression, and problem solving) and intelligence (such as solving arithmetic problems and learning to use language and to read)?

_____

_____

_____

_____

_____

_____

_____

_____

2. What sorts of diary or interview questions could you ask that would get at the same issues?

_____

_____

_____

_____

_____

_____

_____

3. Where in a home would you leave a tape recorder so that it would record those instances of the target behaviors that are most relevant to your questions?

_____

_____

_____

_____

_____

4. What codes might you subject the tapes to?

_____

_____

_____

_____

_____

_____

GLOSSARY

Direct observational measures: Observations that are conducted live in the field; contrast with indirect methods.
Give your examples:

_____

_____

_____

Indirect observational measures: Data that are collected from participants (e.g., from diaries or logs or from telephone interviews) rather than from direct observations.
   Give your examples:

Rating scale: A type of response item used in a questionnaire or interview in which the responders gives answers in terms of degree.
   Give your examples:

Rating scale, cumulative points: A form of rating scale in which the responder checks one or many responses and the sum of those responses is the unit of analysis.
   Give your examples:

Rating scale, forced choice: A form of rating scale in which a responder must give only one response.

Give your example:

_____

_____

_____

_____

_____

_____

Rating scale, graphic: A form of rating scale in which a response is displayed along a horizontal or vertical line.

Give your example:

_____

_____

_____

_____

_____

_____

Rating scale, numerical: A form of rating scale in which one response is made and the responses lie along a continuum of degree.

Give your example:

_____

_____

_____

_____

_____

Rating scale, standard: A rating scale in which the responses are along a standard criteria, for example, along criteria of percentage.
    Give your example:

_____

_____

_____

_____

Recency of memory: A situation in which a responder provides information that has occurred most recently rather than information that may be more representative.
    Give your example:

_____

_____

_____

_____

Social desirability: Information that participants think the interviewer wants to hear, rather than accurate information.
    Give your example:

_____

_____

_____

_____

12

Using Observational Methods in Educational Settings

THE BEGINNING OF THE END

The theme of this book has been the use of behavioral observations to understand children in their everyday habitats. These habitats include home, school, playgrounds, day-care centers, camps, and numerous other settings where children spend their time. I have noted repeatedly that most of the descriptions of children available to us are of children in schools, preschools, and day-care centers. These descriptions provide important information for educators and parents in terms of the design, implementation, and evaluation of educational programs (see Pellegrini, 1992). Although these descriptions of children in various school settings are important, descriptions of children in other settings are also important, as Wright (1960) noted more than 30 years ago. After all, children spend much of their time in those other places, yet we know very little about them. It is probably the case that knowledge of what children enjoy doing and what they are capable of doing in these diverse settings is useful information for educators. Descriptive information about children's competence in everyday settings can serve as a base for educational programs; this is the core of this final chapter.

In this chapter I cobble together the different pieces of information presented in this book into a statement about implications for observing children in various settings, particularly educational settings. Most basically, observational methods are useful to the degree that they provide valid descriptions of children in various settings. This information can be used in program development, implementation, and evaluation. These points are developed more fully in this chapter.

A PRIMARY BENEFIT OF OBSERVATION

In the very first chapters of this book, I discussed the ways in which observational methods were useful and how they could provide unique forms of information.

Perhaps the clearest and most unique way in which observational methods can be used is to provide good descriptions. Good descriptions—that is, reliable and valid descriptions—in my opinion are the basis of all systematic inquiry. Describing behaviors in terms of physical characteristics and consequences provides important and objective information by which we assign meaning to behavior. For example, we can make inferences about the functions of a behavior by examining its consequence.

Reliable and valid descriptions are also important as a basis for the advancement of knowledge and scholarly interchange. Clear and replicable descriptions of behaviors and their assignment to categories are crucial points in any scientific venture: Clearly stated descriptions invite replication (Blurton Jones, 1972). Convergence between different researchers is an important indicator of the objectivity of our findings. This level of description is necessary before we can do other types of research, educational intervention, or evaluation. If we do not have clear descriptions, we probably do not have clear categories; without such clarity we cannot design studies with meaningful variables. By extension, without clearly stated and objective categories we cannot design meaningful educational programs and evaluation strategies. For example, if we want to implement a play-oriented curriculum in a preschool or use play as an evaluation construct, we first need clear descriptions of play. Without this, how would we proceed? If we cannot define play, we cannot define the basis of our curriculum. Such a description, then, is necessary to design the components of a curriculum and the criteria on which it will be evaluated.

EDUCATORS AS RESEARCHERS AND OBSERVERS

Although all of this sounds simple and obvious, it is absent from much of the research and program evaluation literature that is published. Not very often, for example, do we base components of educational programs on observations of children and teachers. All too often, educators are told what to implement and how to implement various curricula. In many cases curricula are adopted by educational systems based on packages developed by a publishing company or advocated by an educational entrepreneur who visits a school. The assumption behind many of these packaged approaches is that a good idea can be applied almost anywhere. It is developed by a group of "experts" and then sold to very different groups of users.

Indeed, there are numerous problems with such approaches to program development, most notably that these programs often have little or no empirical basis. I argue that in order to be effective, educational programs must be localized and based on the specific characteristics of the children, their families, the educators, and the immediate community. Furthermore, the fact that the teachers themselves are generating the curriculum may have added benefits. Good teaching involves looking at children and figuring out a program for that specific group, based on the specific needs of the children and teachers; thus, packaged programs for the most part are not applicable. When teachers do the important theoretical and empirical work of describing children and using these descriptions as bases for programs, not only are the programs better for children (to the extent that they are tailor made), but the teachers are empowered. This concept of empowerment as applied to educational and family programs (see Cochran & Woolever, 1983, for an extended discussion of this issue in family programs) is similar to the notion of self efficacy. As teachers become more confident that their work is important, they become better teachers. Thus, observational methods can be important vehicles for teachers to develop their own curricula based on the needs of their group and themselves.

Observational methods are an integral and basic part of the movement to empower teachers. Simply put, what children are taught should be based on what teachers know about children; this should be based on descriptions of children in areas that they find interesting and, consequently, in which they exhibit competence. Teachers spend the most time with children in schools and should have an important role in generating these descriptions and curricula.

The extent to which instructional programs are implemented and modified, in turn, needs description. These descriptions should provide important information on the interface between individual teachers and individual children who are participating in educational programs. All too often, educators are presented with programs to implement. Not very often, however, are they informed of the degree to which the program is being implemented. Clearly, we cannot assume that a program is being implemented in a uniform way across different teachers and schools. Observational methods are excellent methods for this sort of process description.

Finally, good descriptions can and should be used in evaluation of the educational program. By evaluation, I mean systematic documentation of the ways in which educational programs affect teachers, children, and families. Typically, educators make inferences about program impact based on tests or questionnaires. A more direct method of assessment involves using observations to complement these other forms of assessment. For example, in evaluating children's achievement it makes sense to have a variety of data, including test scores, children's work samples, and behavioral observations. Similarly, when assessing teacher effectiveness, direct observations should be complemented with lesson plans, student evaluations, and teacher performance tests. Given the importance of observations in schools and the corresponding time demands, it might be helpful for school systems to provide specific training in observational methods for evaluation personnel (I acknowledge Don Ratcliff for this idea).

OBSERVATIONAL DESCRIPTIONS AND EDUCATIONAL PROGRAMS

I propose that observational descriptions of children in context should provide a basis for educational programming. This proposition is certainly not novel; it has its roots in the child study movement from the turn of the century. From at least the time of Darwin, Dewey, Piaget, and Vygotsky, and more recently Kohlberg and Cole, the child study movement has advocated that educational programs should have, as a starting point, a thorough understanding of children. This is accomplished by compiling detailed observations, which are, in turn, used as bases for program curriculum, instruction, and evaluation. This child-centered approach contrasts with other approaches to educational programs, such as the "structure of the discipline" approach, in which programs for children are based on adult models of a subject matter field, like mathematics or biology. My bias is that we should not consider subject matter independent of children, just as we should not consider individuals independent of context. Children as they interact in schools should be the basis of any curriculum.

Observations as Bases for Educational Programs

The traditional components of educational programs involve a needs assessment, development of materials and instructional strategies, and evaluation procedures. Although this framework may be useful, I suggest that we focus this process on describing children, which should be the basis of our program. In this section, I outline how descriptions can be used as a basis of curriculum and instruction.

The idea is that educators should take as a starting point things that are interesting to children and, consequently, those areas in which children are likely to exhibit competence. Children are most likely to exhibit high levels of competence in areas in which they are interested, compared to those areas in which they are in minimally interested (Waters & Sroufe, 1983). For example, compare the levels of linguistic competence exhibited by preschool children when they are engaged in fantasy play with their peers to the competence they exhibit when they are taking a standardized test. Children are more likely to exhibit higher levels of competence in enjoyable situations because those situations may demand high levels in order for the child to participate.

The initial job of educators is to locate those dimensions of children's lives that the children find exciting and that are also intellectually challenging. This search process may be particularly important if children's home experiences differ from teachers' and schools' expectations. Here, obviously, observational methods are useful: they can be used to locate situations that are familiar and motivating to children. Again, these ideas date at least as far back as Dewey, but it is not a trivial task to locate those important contexts that can be used as bases for educational programs. Certainly, the use of a combination of indirect and direct observational methods, as suggested in Chapter 11, is a starting point. I have addressed in other places the way this process can work with developing mathematics curriculum for young children (Pellegrini & Stanic, 1993). Here, I briefly outline an example of using observational methods to locate children's indigenous mathematical competence. This competence, in turn, could be the basis of a school mathematics curriculum.

Choosing to redesign a school mathematics curriculum is important to the extent that American children, in comparison to children from Japan and Taiwan, have difficulty with mathematics. Thus, it would be useful to know where, outside of school, children exhibit mathematical competence. If we can locate these areas of competence, they can be used to complement the school mathematics curriculum.

Locating competence can be accomplished in a two-step process. First, using indirect observational measures, we could sample where, with whom, and with what children engage in activities involving mathematical operations such as counting, making greater than or less than judgments, and establishing one-to-one correspondences. This can be done most readily by leaving diaries with children's caregivers, who would record the relevant information. As noted in both Chapters 10 and 11, diary entries are most reliable when specific information is requested. We could specify, as in Fig. 12.1, the specific contexts of interest.

The information provided by daily diaries or logs can be used to identify those times and places where live behavioral observations should be conducted. Taking the data from Fig. 12.1, we could conduct direct observations of children's exhibition of counting knowledge observing the focal children as they go up and down stairs at school. We could even use this information later in the evaluation aspect of the process to design a task to assess children's knowledge of counting. The indirect measures tell us where these processes can be observed and the direct observations tell us about the social processes involved in counting, for example, that counting may be embedded in a song. In terms of using this information for curriculum design, we might then say that one way in which counting can be taught is by having children sing counting songs.

Observations and Program Implementation

The next level of the educational process involves determining the extent to which programs are being implemented. That is, assume that we have an educational program that is composed of a variety of materials, activities, and interactional

Child: Sarah Smith   Date: June 6

	Where	*When*	*With What*	*With Whom*	*Example of Behavior*
Counting:					
1.	Stairs/school	7:30 am	Walking up	Mother	1, 2, 3 stairs
Entered by Mother					
2.	Stairs/school	2:30 pm	Walking down	Babysitter	1, 2, 3 stairs
Entered by Babysitter					
3.	His bedroom	3 pm	Legos	Babysitter	1, 2, 3, 5
Entered by Babysitter					
1:1:					
</>:					
4.	Restaurant	7 pm	Ice cream	Brother	"You have more"
Entered by Father					

FIG. 12.1   Diary entry for locating mathematical competence.

strategies. We should use observational methods to determine the degree to which the materials are actually being implemented. We might also complement this information by identifying those processes that differentiate successful and unsuccessful implementation. The observational methods relevant to this aspect of the educational process involve observing the degree to which individual teachers and children implement the program. The behavioral categories include aspects of the program such as singing counting games as well as other relevant aspects identified through indirect and direct methods.

This sort of process data, or information on program implementation, is invaluable in all educational programs because it helps define what is implemented. The level of actual implementation is often different from the level of stated implementation. It may be helpful to think of these process data as content validity data on the program. We can claim content validity if our construct (in this case, the program) measures what it purports to measure. Our program would be content valid if it were implemented according to the program criteria.

Too often we only know about programs as they are described on paper. We generally do not know the extent to which these stated goals correspond to the implementation of the program goals. Given the variability in teachers' and children's willingness and ability to implement different programs, it is very questionable that there is much correspondence between stated and actual program descriptors. That is, what goes on in most programs probably does not correspond very closely to the formal program descriptions.

Another use of process data relates to the evaluation dimension. We could explore the links between aspects of program implementation and children's achievement. For example, we might have increasing children's counting games on the playground as a goal of our program. We could identify those aspects of the program that empirically predict counting games at recess. The activities that maximize gains could be increased in the classroom, whereas those that minimize gains could be phased out in favor of new ones. The new activities, of course, should be derived from the first phase of this process.

Observations and Program Evaluation

Evaluation in education is currently increasing in frequency. Simultaneously, it is under great scrutiny. Teachers and students in the U.S. and the United Kingdom, to take only two examples, are under increased demand to exhibit their competence, performance, knowledge and so on. Traditionally, the format for students and teachers to exhibit their knowledge or skills has been the paper and pencil test. Performance on these tests may or may not be empirically related to the desired outcome; that is, the tests may or may not have criterion validity. For example, some states require that teachers pass a test on their knowledge of teaching methods in order to be certified. In other cases, children must pass a standardized test in order to be promoted from one grade to another. In most cases there is little empirical evidence to show that a specified level of performance on a test relates to desired outcome, like performance in the next grade. It is not clear what determines an adequate score or how levels of adequacy are determined. This type of testing is increasing for both teachers and students despite such gaping problems.

There are, however, concerns being voiced in the educational community over these testing practices (e.g., Gardner, 1993). The fact that scores on these measures tell us little about actual levels of competence or performance may have something to do with the concern. For many years, standardized forms of testing have been criticized as being nonmotivating and intimidating for the test takers. Moreover, the content and format of the test questions often do not measure the degree to which information is used or can be used by the test taker.

It is in this realm that observational methods have something very important to offer. If we specify clearly what it is we want to measure, say the different types of mathematical competence discussed previously, we can design analogue situations and then observe the extent to which children use these concepts in the classroom. There is little need to transfer from the assessment context to the use of the concepts in school contexts: Children are being assessed as they are using the concept. Furthermore, the assessment situation should be minimally intimidating to children to the extent that they are being assessed in their own classrooms on familiar and interesting tasks. From a motivational perspective, if we design classroom evaluation tasks with an eye on what interests children, the children should exhibit maximum levels of competence. Thus, observing children in motivating classroom situations is an ideal assessment context.

This concept of the motivating classroom evaluation task also allows us to use observational methods to get at children's underlying competence, an area often claimed solely by test developers. Their argument went something like this. If we are interested in knowing how much mathematics a child knows, we should ask the child directly about those aspects of mathematics that we think are important. We should not rely on naturalistic observations of children in order to make judgments about children's competence because (arguments of economy of time aside, for the time being) a child may choose not to exhibit competence when he or she is being observed. To minimize this sampling problem, test items are written to ask children about things about which we want to know; thus, the test item is the context for children to exhibit knowledge.

The problem with the argument is that the test questions are not motivating to many children, especially young children. This problem is part of the reason that young children are unreliable test takers (Messick, 1983). Furthermore, observational methods can address these elusive aspects of competence: If we observe children in tasks that are motivating, the children should want to exhibit high levels of competence. Is it accidental that preschool children often exhibit higher levels of language and representational processes in peer discourse events, such as fantasy play, than in more traditional assessment contexts (Cazden, 1975; Pellegrini, 1992)? Children may exhibit higher levels of competence in fantasy play than on tests because they find fantasy motivating and want to participate in the fantasy process. Because fantasy play with peers requires high levels of linguistic and representational competence to be sustained, children bring all their social cognitive processes to the fore to participate in this motivating process. The trick is to design instructional and evaluation tasks that are meaningful, motivating, and intellectually demanding for children.

Using observational techniques for the design and evaluation of educational programs does have a down side, which relates to economy. It should be all too evident that conducting observations is very expensive. It takes numerous hours to gather reliable and valid information about children. Actually, this is the argument proffered by many administrators in favor of testing. Although observation is more expensive than testing, it often provides better, or at least good, complementary information; it is certainly less expensive than school failure.

THINGS TO THINK ABOUT

1. List some indirect observational methods that can be used to answer the following questions:

1a. Where do children spend most of their out-of-school time?

_____

_____

_____

_____

_____

_____

_____

_____

1b. With whom is it spent? Doing what?

_____

_____

_____

_____

_____

_____

_____

_____

1c. Where, with whom, and how do young children use reading and writing at home?

_____

_____

_____

_____

_____

_____

_____

1d. What resources are provided by these forms of literacy?

_____

_____

_____

_____

_____

_____

_____

2. Whom might you interview to obtain answers to these questions?

_____

_____

_____

_____

_____

_____

_____

_____

_____

3. Write some sample questions.

_____

_____

_____

_____

_____

_____

4. Having gathered information on these indirect measures, what direct observation sampling and recording rules would you use to answer questions 1a, 1b, and 1c?

_____

_____

_____

_____

_____

5. What are some possible classroom activities that could serve as evaluation activities?

6. How might a teacher get help in conducting the expensive work of direct observations?

7. How can direct observational measures be used to replace traditional testing methods? How can they be used to complement traditional methods?

_____

_____

_____

_____

_____

_____

_____

GLOSSARY

Context: The physical and social situation in which individuals are embedded. Give your example:

_____

_____

_____

_____

Empowerment: The process by which teachers and children gain a sense of worth and power in their abilities to teach and learn, respectively. Empowerment is often a result of taking an active role in charting the course of educational programs. Give your example:

_____

_____

_____

Explanatory statements: Statements that make causal connections among propositions; for example, "Sugar causes children to be hyperactive."
Give your example:

_____

_____

_____

_____

Process data: The descriptive information on the implementation of educational programs. For example, to what degree do teachers ask the sorts of questions specified by a program?
Give your example:

_____

_____

_____

_____

Self-efficacy: Feelings of self-worth accomplishment.
Give your example:

_____

_____

_____

_____

_____

Transaction: The reciprocal influence of two entities on each other; for example, the influences of people and environments on each other.
   Give your example:

_____

_____

_____

_____

Transfer: The degree to which information from one setting can be applied to another. In this chapter, I discussed the degree to which information about children's knowledge as measured by a test transferred to their use of that knowledge in the classroom.
   Give your example:

_____

_____

_____

_____

References

Altmann, J. (1974). Observational study of behavior: Sampling methods. *Behavior, 49,* 227–265.

Applebaum, M., & McCall, R. (1983). Design and analysis in developmental research. In W. Kessen (Ed.), *Handbook of child psychology,* Vol. 1 (pp. 415–476). New York: Wiley.

Bakeman, R., & Gottman, J. (1986). *Observing interaction.* New York: Cambridge University Press.

Bakeman, R., & Quera, V. (in preparation). *Analyzing interaction.*

Barker, R. (1968). *Ecological psychology.* Stanford: Stanford University Press.

Barker, R., & Wright, H. (1955). *Midwest and its children.* San Francisco: Jossey-Bass.

Bloch, M. (1989). Young boys' and girls' play at home and in the community: A cultural-ecological framework. In M. Bloch & A. D. Pellegrini (Eds.), *The ecological context of children's play* (pp. 120–154). Norwood, NJ: Ablex.

Blurton Jones, N. (1972). Characteristics of ethological studies of human behaviour. In N. Blurton Jones (Ed.), *Ethological studies of child behaviour* (pp. 3–36). Cambridge, England: Cambridge University Press.

Boccia, M. (1992, March). Product review: The observer. *Bulletin of the American Society of Primatologists.*

Braunwald, S., & Brislin, R. (1979). The diary method updated. In E. Ochs & B. Schieffelin (Eds.), *Developmental pragmatics* (pp. 21–42). New York: Academic Press.

Bronfenbrenner, U. (1979). *The ecology of human development.* Cambridge, MA: Harvard University Press.

Burts, D., Hart, C., Charleworth, R., Fleege, P., Mosely, J., & Thomasson, R. (1992). Observed activities and stress behaviors of children in developmentally inappropriate kindergarten classrooms. *Early Childhood Research Quarterly, 7,* 297–318.

Cairns, R., & Cairns, B. (1986). An evolutionary and developmental perspective on aggression. In C. Zahn-Waxler, E. Cummings, & R. Iannoti (Eds.), *Altruism and aggression* (pp. 58–87). New York: Cambridge University Press.

Caldwell, B., & Bradley, R. (1984). *The HOME inventory.* Little Rock: University of Arkansas.

Cazden, C. B. (1975). Hypercorrection in test responses. *Theory Into Practice, 14,* 343–346.

Cheyney, D., & Seyfarth, R. (1990). *How monkeys see the world.* Chicago: University of Chicago Press.

Cochran, M., & Woolever, F. (1983). Beyond the deficit model: The empowerment of parents with information and informational support. In I. Sigel & L. Laosa (Eds.), *Changing families* (pp. 225–246). New York: Plenum.

Cole, M. (1993, March). *A cultural-historical goal for developmental research.* Paper presented at the biennial meetings of the Society for Research in Child Development, New Orleans.

Corsaro, W. (1981). Entering the child's world. In J. Green & C. Wallat (Eds.), *Ethnography and language in educational settings* (pp. 117–146). Norwood, NJ: Ablex.

Cronbach, L. (1957). The two disciplines of psychology. *American Psychology, 12,* 671–684.

Cronbach, L. (1980). Validity on parole: How can we go straight? In D. Fisk & R. Shweder (Eds.), *New directions for testing and measurement* (pp. 99–108). San Francisco: Jossey-Bass.

Cronbach, L., Gleser, G., Nanda, H., & Rajaratnam, N. (1972). *The dependability of behavioral measurement.* New York: Wiley.

Csikszentmihalyi, M. (1990). *Flow: The psychology of optimal experience.* New York: Harper & Row.

Dansky, J. & Silverman, I. (1973) Effects of play on associative fluency in preschool age children. *Developmental Psychology, 9,* 38–42.

Dansky, J. & Silverman, I. (1975). Play: A general facilitation of associative fluency. *Developmental Psychology, 11,* 104.

Darwin, C. (1877). Biographical sketch of an infant. *Mind, 2,* 285–294.

Dickinson, D., & Moreton, J. (1991, April). *Predicting specific kindergarten literacy skills from three-year-olds' preschool experience*. Paper presented at the biennial meetings of the Society for Research in Child Development, Seattle.

Dunn, J. (1988). *The beginnings of social understanding*. Cambridge, MA: Harvard University Press.

Dunn, J. (1993). *Young children's close relationships*. Beverly Hills, CA: Sage.

Evertson, C., & Green, J. (1986). Observation as inquiry and method. In M. Wittrock (Ed.), *Handbook of research on teaching* (pp. 162–213). New York: Macmillan.

Fine, G., & Sandstrom, K. (1988). *Knowing children: Participant observation*. Beverly Hills, CA: Sage.

Galda, L., Shockley, B., Pellegrini, A., & Stahl, S. (1995). Sharing lives: Reading, writing, and talking in a first grade classroom. *Language Arts, 72*, 334–339.

Gardner, H. (1993). *Multiple intelligences: The theory in practice*. New York: Basic Books.

Gottman, J., & Roy, A. (1990). *Sequential analysis*. New York: Cambridge University Press.

Guilford, J., & Fruchter, B. (1973). *Fundamental statistics in psychology and education*. New York: McGraw-Hill.

Gump, P. (1989). Ecological psychology and issues of play. In M. Bloch & A. Pellegrini (Eds.), *The ecological contexts of children's play* (pp. 35–56). Norwood, NJ: Ablex.

Heath, S. (1983). *Ways with words*. New York: Cambridge University Press.

Heath, S. (with H. Chin). (1985). Narrative play in second language learning. In L. Galda & A. Pellegrini (Eds.), *Play, language, and stories* (pp. 147–166). Norwood, NJ: Ablex.

Herbert, J., & Attridge, C. (1975). A guide for developers and users of observation systems and manuals. *American Educational Research Journal, 12*, 1–20.

Hille, M. (1991). Hand-held behavioral observations: The Observer. *Behavioral Assessment, 13*, 187–188.

Hinde, R. (1973). On the design of check-sheets. *Primates, 14*, 393–406.

Hinde, R. (1980). *Ethology*. London: Fontana.

Hollander, M., & Wolfe, D. (1973). *Nonparametric statistical methods*. New York: Wiley.

Hollenbeck, A. (1978). Problems of reliability in observational research. In G. Sackett (Ed.), *Observing behavior*, Vol. 1 (pp. 79–98). Baltimore: University Park Press.

Hymes, D. (1980). *Langauge in education: Ethnolinguistic essays*. Washington, DC: Center for Applied Linguistics.

Kagan, J. (1994). On the nature of emotion. In N. Fox (Ed.), The development of emotion regulation: Biological and behavioral considerations. *Monographs for the Society for Research in Child Development, 59*, 1–2. Serial No. 240.

Kerlinger, F. (1973). *Foundations of behavioral research*. New York: Holt, Rinehart & Winston.

Leger, D., & Didrichson, I. (1994). An assessment of data pooling and some alternatives. *Animal Behaviour, 48*, 823–832.

Linn, R. (1994). Performance assessment: Policy promises and technical measurement standards. *Educational Researcher, 23*, 4–14.

Loevenger, J. (1957). Objective tests as instruments of psychological theory. *Psychological Reports, 3*, 635–694.

Lykken, D. (1970). Statistical significance in psychological research. *Psychological Bulletin, 70*, 151–159.

Martin, P., & Bateson, P. (1993). *Measuring behavior*. Cambridge, England: Cambridge University Press.

McCall, R. (1977). Challenges to a science of developmental psychology. *Child Development, 48*, 333–394.

McCall, R. (1980). *Fundamental statistics for psychology*. New York: Harcourt Brace.

Mead, M. (1954). Research on primative children. In L. Carmichael (Ed.), *Manual of child psychology* (pp. 735–780). New York: Wiley.

Messick, S. (1975). The standard problem: Meaning and values in measurement and evaluation. *American Psychologist, 30*, 1012–1027.

Messick, S. (1983). Assessment of children. In W. Kessen (Ed.), *Handbook of child psychology*, Vol. 1 (pp. 477–526). New York: Wiley.

Moss, P. (1992). Shifting conceptions of validity in educational measurement: Implications for performance assessment. *Review of Educational Research, 62*, 229–258.

Norusis, M. (1988a). *SPSS/PC+ advanced statistics V2.0*. Chicago: SPSS, Inc.

Norusis, M. (1988b). *SPSS/PC+ studentware*. Chicago: SPSS, Inc.

Packer, M. (1985). Hermeneutic inquiry in the study of human conduct. *American Psychology, 16*, 1081–1093.

Patterson, G. (1982). *Coercive family processes*. Eugene, OR: Castalia.

Patton, M. (1990). *Qualitative evaluation and research methods*. Beverly Hills, CA: Sage.

Pellegrini, A. D. (1992). *Applied child study: A developmental approach*. Hillsdale, NJ: Lawrence Erlbaum Associates.

Pellegrini, A. D. (1993). Boys' rough-and-tumble play, social competence, and group composition. British *Journal of Developmental Psychology, 11*, 237–248.

Pellegrini, A. D. (1995). *School recess and playground behavior*. Albany, NY: State University of New York Press.

Pellegrini, A. D., Brody, G., & Sigel, I. (1985). Parents' bookreading habits with their children. *Journal of Educational Psychology, 77*, 332–340.

Pellegrini, A. D., & Davis, P. (1993). Relations between children's playground and classroom behavior. British *Journal of Educational Psychology, 63*, 88–95.

Pellegrini, A. D., & Galda, L. (1991). Longitudinal relations among symbolic play, metalinguistic verbs, and emergent literacy. In J. Christie (Ed.), *Play and early literacy development* (pp. 47–68). Albany, NY: State University of New York Press.

Pellegrini, A. D., Galda, L., Shockley, B., & Stahl, S. (1995). The nexus of social and literacy experiences at home and at school: Implications for primary school oral language and literacy. *British Journal of Educational Psychology, 65*, 273–285.

Pellegrini, A. D., Huberty, P. D., & Jones, I. (1995). The effects of recess timing on children's playground and clasroom behaviors. *American Educational Research Journal, 32*.

Pellegrini, A. D., & Perlmutter, J. (1989). Classroom contextual effects on children's play. *Developmental Psychology, 25*, 289–296.

Pellegrini, A. D., & Stanic, G. M. A. (1993). Locating children's mathematical competence: Application of the developmental niche. *Journal of Applied Developmental Psychology, 14*, 501–520.

Piaget, J. (1962). *Play, dreams, and imitation in childhood*. New York: Norton.

Pike, K. (1965). *Language in relation to a unified theory of the structure of human behavior*. The Hague: Mouton.

Rubin, K., Fein, G., & Vandenberg, B. (1983). Play. In E. M. Hetherington (Ed.), *Handbook of child psychology*, Vol. 4 (pp. 693–774). New York: Wiley.

Rutter, M., & Garmezy, N. (1983). Developmental psychopathology. In E. M. Hetherington (Ed.), *Handbook of child psychology*, Vol. 4 (pp. 775–912). New York: Wiley.

Sachs, J. (1980). The role of adult–child play in language development. In K. Rubin (Ed.), *Children's play* (pp. 33–48). San Francisco: Jossey-Bass.

Sackett, G. (1978). Measurement in observational research. In G. Sackett (Ed.), *Observing behavior*, Vol. 1 (pp. 25–43). Baltimore: University Park Press.

Sapir, E. (1925). Sound patterns in language. *Language, 1*, 37–51.

Sears, R., Maccoby, E., & Levin, H. (1957). *Patterns of child rearing*. Evanston, IL: Row, Peterson and Co.

Shepard, L. (1993). Psychometricians' views about learning. *Educational Researcher, 20*, 2–16.

Siegel, S. (1956). *Nonparametric statistics for the behavioral sciences*. New York: McGraw-Hill.

Simon, A., & Boyer, G. (1967). (Eds.). *Mirrors for behavior*. Philadelphia: Research For Better Schools.

Simon, T., & Smith, P. K. (1983). The study of play and problem solving in preschool children. *British Journal of Developmental Psychology, 1*, 289–297.

Skinner, B. F. (1974), *About behaviorism*. New York: Vintage.

Sluckin, A. (1981). *Growing up in the playground*. London: Routledge & Kegan Paul.

Smilansky, S. (1968). *The effects of sociodramatic play on economically disadvantaged preschool children*. New York: Wiley.

Smith, P. K. (1985). The reliability and validity of one-zero sampling. *British Educational Research Journal, 11*, 215–220.

Smith, P. K., & Connolly, K. (1980). *The ecology of preschool behaviour*. Cambridge, England: Cambridge University Press.

Smith, P. K., & Hagan, T. (1980). Effects of play deprivation on exercise play in nursery school children. *Animal Behavior, 28*, 922–928.

Smith, P. K., & Whitney, S. (1987). Play and associative fluency: Experimenter effects may be responsible for previous findings. *Developmental Psychology, 23*, 49–53.

Snow, C. (1983). Literacy and language: Relationships during the preschool years. *Harvard Educational Review, 53*, 165–189.

Suen, H., & Ary, D. (1989). *Analyzing quantitative behavioral observation data*. Hillsdale, NJ: Lawrence Erlbaum Associates.

Super, C., & Harkness, S. (1986). The developmental niche. *International Journal of Behavioral Development, 9*, 545–569.

Sylva, K., Bruner, J., & Genoa, P. (1976). The role of play on problem solving in children 3–5 years old. In J. Bruner, A. Jally, & K. Sylva (Eds.). *Play—Its role in development and evolution* (pp. 244–261) New York: Basic Books.

Tamis-Lemonde, C., Kahana-Kalman, R., Damast, A., & Bornstein, M. (1992, April). *Associations between patterns of language acquisition and symbolic play across the first two years*. Poster presented at the conference of human development, Atlanta, GA.

Terrill, R. (1973). *R. H. Tawney and his times*. Cambridge, MA: Harvard University Press.

Tinbergen, N. (1963). On the aims and methods of ethology. *Z. Tierpsycholo, 20*, 410–433.

Tizard, B., & Hughes, M. (1983). *Young children learning*. Cambridge, MA: Harvard University Press.

Tomasello, M. (1993). *First verbs*. New York: Cambridge University Press.

Tourtellot, M. (1992). Review of The Observer. *Journal of Insect Behavior, 5*, 415–416.

Vandenberg, B. (1980). Play, problem solving, and creativity. In K. Rubin (Ed.), *Children's play* (pp. 49–68). San Francisco: Jossey-Bass.

Wachs, T. (1985, April). *Measurement of environment in the study of organism environment interaction*. Paper presented at the biennial meetings of the Society for the Research in Child Development, Toronto.

Waters, E., & Sroufe, L. A. (1983). Social competence as a developmental construct. *Developmental Review, 3*, 79–97.

Wells, G. (1985). *Language development in the preschool years*. Cambridge, England: Cambridge University Press.

Wright, H. (1960). Observational child study. In P. Mussen (Ed.), *Handbook of research methods in child development* (pp. 71–139). New York: Wiley.

Author Index

Subject Index

5627